ANTONIO BUERO VALLEJO

by Martha T. Halsey

The première of Antonio Buero Vallejo's *Historia de una escalera* (*Story of a Stairway*) gave new direction and vitality to the Spanish theater after the Civil War of 1936-39. It incorporates a tragic portrayal of human existence generally missing from the Spanish stage of the twentieth century. Its impact upon the theater is comparable to that produced by Camilo José Cela's *La familia de Pascual Duarte* (*The Family of Pascual Duarte*) upon the novel or Dámaso Alonso's *Hijos de la ira* (*Sons of Wrath*) upon poetry. Since 1949, Buero, who is now recognized as Spain's foremost dramatist, has written many types of plays. Some evince the social emphasis of his theater and others gravitate toward a metaphysical pole. However, in all, a tendency toward the tragic is a basic element.

The present study examines Buero's critical essays on the theater and analyzes his dramas in the light of the theories Buero expresses in an attempt to elucidate his dramatic art. It attempts, finally, to clarify Buero's unique significance to the reconstruction of twentieth-century Spanish theater.

TWAYNE'S WORLD AUTHORS SERIES

A Survey of the World's Literature

Sylvia E. Bowman, Indiana University

GENERAL EDITOR

SPAIN

Gerald Wade, Vanderbilt University

EDITOR

Antonio Buero Vallejo

(TWAS 260)

TWAYNE'S WORLD AUTHORS SERIES (TWAS)

The purpose of TWAS is to survey the major writers —novelists, dramatists, historians, poets, philosophers, and critics—of the nations of the world. Among the national literatures covered are those of Australia, Canada, China, Eastern Europe, France, Germany, Greece, India, Italy, Japan, Latin America, the Netherlands, New Zealand, Poland, Russia, Scandinavia, Spain, and the African nations, as well as Hebrew, Yiddish, and Latin Classical literatures. This survey is complemented by Twayne's United States Authors Series and English Authors Series.

The intent of each volume in these series is to present a critical-analytical study of the works of the writer; to include biographical and historical material that may be necessary for understanding, appreciation, and critical appraisal of the writer; and to present all material in clear, concise English—but not to vitiate the scholarly content of the work by doing so.

Antonio Buero Vallejo

By MARTHA T. HALSEY
The Pennsylvania State University

ABOUT THE AUTHOR

Martha T. Halsey is Associate Professor of Spanish at The Pennsylvania State University. She received her B.A. from Goucher College, her M.A.
from the University of Iowa, and her Ph.D. from
The Ohio State University. She formerly taught at
Iowa State University and The Ohio State University. Professor Halsey's specialty is contemporary Spanish drama, and she has contributed
articles and reviews on the theater to *Hispania,
Romance Notes, Revista de Estudios Hispánicos,
Comparative Literature Studies, Contemporary Literature, Kentucky Romance Quarterly,* and the
Romanic Review. She is co-editor of an edition of
Buero's *Madrugada,* published by Ginn and Co.,
and an editorial associate for the journal *Modern
International Drama.*

York

To the Memory of my Father

Preface

The Spanish stage has been slow to recover from the effects of the Civil War of 1936-1939. The major attempt at reconstruction in recent years has been that represented by Antonio Buero Vallejo. Despite initial hostility because of his Republican background and his intellectual independence, a rigid system of government censorship, and the prevalent commercialization of the Spanish stage, Buero has refused to make concessions of either an ideological or economic nature. It is largely through his efforts that tragedy has been restored to its proper place in Spanish theater. For these reasons Buero has emerged as Spain's foremost living dramatist. The serious and responsible direction he has given the contemporary Spanish stage is now being followed by a new generation of playwrights who grew up during the Civil War: Alfonso Sastre, Carlos Muñiz, Ricardo Buded, and Lauro Olmo.

The present study of Buero's theater is intended to elucidate the substance of his thought and dramatic art. Buero's plays will be analyzed in the light of his theories on the theater in general, and on tragedy in particular, which he has expressed in numerous critical essays and which the author has discussed with him on several occasions, including his visit to The Pennsylvania State University in 1966. No book has yet been published on Buero's entire theater to date. The author hopes that her work will serve to introduce one of Spain's most significant literary figures to new English-speaking readers and that it will also prove of some interest to American specialists in Spain's contemporary theater.

The discussion of Buero's earlier plays is based on a 1964 doctoral dissertation done at The Ohio State University and translations, unless otherwise indicated, are the author's.

Martha T. Halsey

The Pennsylvania State University

Acknowledgments

The author wishes to thank the American Philosophical Society for a grant which made possible research for this study of Buero's theater. She also wishes to express her appreciation to Professors Robert Lima and Anthony M. Pasquariello and to editor Gerald Wade for their helpful criticism.

Contents

Chronology

1916   September 29: Buero Vallejo born in Guadalajara, Spain.

1934   Buero enrolls in the San Fernando School of Fine Arts in Madrid.

1936   Spanish Civil War begins; Buero works in the Office of Information of the *Federación Universitaria Escolar* (University Student Federation), a democratic student association, then serves in the infantry of the Republican forces, and later, in the Medical Corps (Sanidad Militar).

1939   At the end of the Civil War, Buero receives the death sentence, which is later commuted to a prison sentence.

1946   After Buero is released from prison, he begins to write his early plays, starting with *En la ardiente oscuridad* (*In the Burning Darkness*).

1949   Buero's *Las palabras en la arena* (*The Words in the Sand*) awarded the Friends of the Quinteros Award and *Historia de una escalera* (*Story of a Stairway*) receives the Lope de Vega Prize. October 14: Première of *Story of a Stairway* at the Español Theater in Madrid. December 19: Première of *The Words in the Sand* at the Español Theater.

1950   December 1: Première of *In the Burning Darkness* at the María Guerrero Theater in Madrid.

1952   January 11: Première of *La tejedora de sueños* (*The Dream Weaver*) at the Español Theater. May 21: *La señal que se espera* (*The Awaited Sign*) premières at the Infanta Isabel in Madrid.

1953   January 10: *Casi un cuento de hadas* (*Almost a Fairy Tale*) premières at the Alcázar Theater in Madrid. December 9: *Madrugada* (*Dawn*) premières at the Alcázar.

1954   The Censor's office prohibits the première of *Aventura en lo gris* (*Adventure in Gray*). It is published in the journal *Teatro*, in Madrid. December 14: *Irene ó el tesoro* (*Irene or the Treasure*) at the María Guerrero.

1956   September 20: *Hoy es fiesta* (*Today's a Holiday*) premières at the María Guerrero. It is awarded the María Rolland Prize for 1956.

1957   November 5: *Las cartas boca abajo* (*The Cards Face Down*) premières at the Reina Victoria Theater in Madrid. *Today's* a Holiday is awarded the National Theater Prize for 1957. Buero is denied an exit visa to attend the opening of one of his plays in France.

1958 December 18: *Un soñador para un pueblo* (*A Dreamer for a People*) premières at the Español and is awarded the María Rolland Prize for 1958. *The Cards Face Down* receives the National Theater Prize for 1958.

1959 Buero marries the actress Victoria Rodríguez at Madrid's San Sebastián Church. *Today's a Holiday* is awarded the March Foundation Prize for 1959. *A Dreamer for a People* receives the National Theater Prize for 1959.

1960 December 9: Première of *Las Meninas* (*The Ladies-in-Waiting*) at the Español. The play is the recipient of the María Rolland Prize for 1960. *A Dreamer for a People* receives the Critics of Barcelona Award for 1960. Buero is one of 277 Spanish writers who sign a public statement condemning censorship in Spain.

1961 Birth of first son, Carlos. December 14: Buero's version of *Hamlet* performed at the Español.

1962 Birth of second son, Enrique. November 16: Première of *El concierto de San Ovidio* (*Concert at Saint Ovide*) at the Goya Theater in Madrid. It is awarded the Larra Prize for 1961-1962.

1963 October 1: A revised version of *Adventure in Gray* is performed at the Club Recoletos Theater in Madrid. Together with other intellectuals, Buero signs a letter to the government asking for an investigation of the alleged torture of striking miners, and another letter about the same matter with 188 other persons. The government brings charges against them, which are later dropped.

1964 October 29: Buero gives address at the opening session of Unamuno Centennial sponsored by the Friends of UNESCO in Madrid.

1966 March 25-May 31: Buero visits the United States on a State Department tour and delivers lectures on Spanish drama and art at major universities. October 18: Buero elected a Corresponding Member of the Hispanic Society of America. November 8: Buero's version of *Mother Courage and her Children* (*Madre Coraje y sus hijos*) opens at the Bellas Artes Theater in Madrid.

1967 August 26: Buero and his wife travel to San Miniato for the Italian première of *Concert at Saint Ovide*. October 7: Première of *El tragaluz* (*The Basement Window*) at the Bellas Artes Theater. It is awarded the *Spectator and Critic* Prize for 1967.

Chronology

1968   Publication of *Mito: Libro para una ópera* (*Myth: Libreto for an Opera*) in the journal *Primer Acto*. November 22: Buero and wife attend the première of the English version of *La doble historia del doctor Valmy* (*The Double Case History of Doctor Valmy*) at the Gateway Theatre, Chester, England, after performance of the play was not authorized in Spain.

1969   December 29: Buero elected an Honorary Fellow of the American Association of Teachers of Spanish and Portuguese.

1970   February 6: Première of *El sueño de la razón* (*The Sleep of Reason*) at the Reina Victoria Theater. It receives the *Spectator and Critic* Prize for 1970. April 30-May 2: Buero and his wife are guests of honor at a Symposium on the Spanish Theater at the University of North Carolina at Chapel Hill. They later spend some time in New York City and Buero lectures at Barnard College. June 26: Buero reads a paper at the 27th Annual World Congress of Authors in Las Palmas entitled "Problemas del teatro actual" ("Problems of Current Theater"). September 25: Buero and his wife attend the Italian première of *The Sleep of Reason* at the Festival of San Miniato.

1971   February 3: Buero elected to occupy Chair X in the Spanish Royal Academy, left vacant by the death of Rodríguez Moñino.

CHAPTER 1

The Man and His Times

> "The true and honest life is always, in my
> opinion, tragic. Only the person who embraces
> this essential truth, like one who embraces his
> beloved, can attain to the maximum fulfill-
> ment. Similarly, only that theater which gravi-
> tates toward this tremendous truth can aspire
> to become a great theater."
>
> —Buero, "Palabra final," *historia de una
> escalera* ("Final Words," *Story of a
> Stairway*)[1]

I *The Situation After the Spanish Civil War*

THE première of Antonio Buero Vallejo's *Historia de una escalera* (*Story of a Stairway*) in 1949 marked the resurgence of serious Spanish theater after the Civil War (1936-1939). This drama, which describes the hopes and illusions of families in a Madrid tenement, incorporated a tragic portrayal of human existence generally absent from the Spanish stage of the twentieth century. It also served to catapult Spain into the main current of contemporary European theater. Previously the Spanish stage had been dominated by the drawing room comedy of Jacinto Benavente and Gregorio Martínez Sierra and by the humorous plays of the Alvarez Quintero brothers—by a theater of diversion. The more serious theater of Miguel de Unamuno was rarely performed and the dramatic career of Federico García Lorca was terminated by his death at the outbreak of the Civil War. The early postwar years had been characterized by a new type of escape theater, termed "theater of evasion," which renounced any purposeful interpretation of reality in favor of adventures of a strictly imaginative nature.[2]

The 1949-1950 theatrical season represents a turning point in Spanish drama because of the new direction represented by Buero

13

Vallejo. Early in his dramatic career the playwright gave his
diagnosis of, and prescription for, the "crisis" in contemporary
Spanish theater: "We are living through a grave moment in
history, but our theater is not moved by it [...] we are content
with a theater of diversion or of evasion. [...] We need, therefore,
in a special way, the rehabilitation of the 'tragic sense' in
our theater, dead since Lorca, Unamuno and some works of
Benavente."[3]

A "tragic sense of life," as seen in the *Celestina, Don Quijote,*
and the plays of Calderón, as well as the later works of Unamuno
and Lorca is, indeed, basic to Spanish literature. In an essay
called "Cuidado con la amargura" ("Be Careful of Bitterness"),
the dramatist points out that an acceptance of "the tragic" has
been typical of the Spanish people. He states that upon writing
Story of a Stairway, he felt imbued with the joyful and courageous
acceptance of tragedy which has given us the most awesome
works of Hispanic painting and literature: "I attempted to look
at the life of my 'stairway' with the same serene look—unskillful in
my case—with which Velázquez looked at his buffoons and his
infantas; Solana, his prostitutes; Benavente and Lorca, their
peasants; or Baroja, his pariahs."[4] Buero strove, he continues, to
give his play this "positive tragic sense" whose purpose is to
fortify or stimulate the spectators' moral sense, not through dis-
courses or sermons, but through its cathartic virtue—in accord
with the oldest tradition of his people. Thus we see that the
substance of Buero's plays is in accord with the most profoundly
traditional artistic currents of his country—even though he brings
to them advanced theatrical techniques.

II *Buero's Life and Career*

Buero Vallejo was born on September 29, 1916, in Guadalajara,
in New Castile. Surrounded by collections of plays and drama
journals which belonged to his father, a military engineer, Buero
became interested in the theater at an early age. In an interview,
in 1952, with Juan del Sarto, published in *Correo Literario,*
Buero describes himself as a child who was very fond of mimicry,
who fought imaginary battles dressed up as D'Artagnan and
recited "Un castellano leal" ("A Loyal Castilian") and a thousand
other old ballads.[5] In these extraordinary quixotic adventures,

Photograph by Gyenes

ANTONIO BUERO VALLEJO

TWAYNE PUBLISHERS, INC.
31 UNION SQUARE WEST   NEW YORK, N. Y. 10003

words were as important as actions. "It is acting," he states in the interview, "that I remember myself as a child; that was the true beginning of my dramatic vocation. Reading and reciting monologues and dialogues were games of which I never tired." Later, for a period of two years, he played what he calls the most fascinating game of his life with a group of friends. With a table or, sometimes, an entire room as their stage, they sometimes constructed complete towns with houses made of wooden boxes and actors of painted cardboard. Speaking for the actors and moving them about, they improvised such diverse subjects as the three musketeers, Buffalo Bill and the "Wild West," fairy tales, and space trips—"marvelous stories," Buero tells del Sarto, "which made me a playwright although I did not realize it until many years later."

Indeed, as a youth, Buero wanted to be a painter and was deeply interested in Velázquez. Therefore, in 1934, after completing his high school studies in Guadalajara at the age of eighteen, he enrolled in the San Fernando School of Fine Arts in Madrid, where his family had moved by then. Buero still keeps, in his Madrid apartment, two albums of drawings done beginning at age seven, carefully selected and labeled by his father, who encouraged his early interest in art: sketches of cowboys—himself among them—comic-strip heroes, the French Revolution, and the numerous idealistic fantasies of his childhood. Later works include a picture of his friend Miguel Hernández, done in 1940, and a sketch of a scene from *Story of a Stairway,* done before the play was staged. In an interview about his painting published in 1960 in *La Estafeta Literaria,* Buero explains that his taste was eclectic. With characteristic humility, he asserts that when he later abandoned his studies, he was at the realistic stage of the beginner.[6]

In 1936, at the outbreak of the Spanish Civil War, Buero interrupted his studies to enlist on the Republican or Loyalist side as a medic—an experience doubtlessly reflected in the strong antiwar or pacifist sentiment found in his theater. At the conclusion of the war, despite his youth, he was sentenced to death, a sentence commuted to a long prison sentence that was later reduced to six years. Upon his release in 1945, at the age of twenty-nine, Buero evidently found it difficult to resume painting after the long period without practice. Profoundly disillusioned, he renounced his dream of becoming a painter, although he continued to produce enough pictures to scrape together a living and was beginning to be respected professionally. He seems to have come to the realization, around 1946, that his deeper interest had always been the theater.

In a discussion of his own theater published in the journal *Primer Acto* in 1957, Buero states that he feels there exists a special relationship between painting and a certain type of theater. Painting may represent the visual mastering of the exterior of men and of things as a necessary preparation for the subsequent exploration of their inner significance. This would be true in the case of a theater which, regardless of how deeply penetrating it may be, does not lose contact with reality in its immediacy. The dramatist speculates that it is for this reason, perhaps, that he began as a realistic painter. A man with a deeply inquiring mind who reads widely both in philosophy and the popular sciences, Buero declares in *Primer Acto*: "My theater is, naturally, an answer—although precarious—to those permanent questions about the world and life with which I am constantly concerned."[7] It is interesting to note that, in one of his plays, he depicts Velázquez' concern with the significance of light, in his painting, as a quest for the ultimate meaning of reality.

In addition to several articles on problems involved in painting and a substantial critical study of Gustave Doré for the Spanish edition of Baron Charles Davillier's *Viaje por España* (*Trip through Spain*), by 1949 Buero had written several plays. In that year, encouraged by friends, but with little real hope of winning, Buero submitted three of his plays to competitions. His one-act play, *Las palabras en la arena* (*The Words in the Sand*), won the Friends of the Quinteros Award and was later performed in the Español Theater by the students of Speech and Drama at the Madrid Conservatory. More importantly, the Lope de Vega Prize, Spain's most prestigious theater prize which had not been awarded since 1933, was won by Buero's *Story of a Stairway*, a tragedy of three generations of Madrid tenement dwellers written in 1947, which, as Buero himself tells us, contains autobiographical elements.[8] "Without recommendations, sponsors, or influence," the critic Alfredo Marqueríe tells us in his prologue to the play, "honestly—without any of the jury knowing him or even who he was—his works were selected [. . .] as the best of hundreds by known and unknown authors which were submitted to the competitions."[9]

The première of *Story of a Stairway* at the Español Theater, guaranteed by the award, was so successful that the traditional annual performance of Zorrilla's *Don Juan Tenorio* was suspended, as the result of public demand, so as not to interrupt its run. The work established Buero's reputation as the first serious dramatist of social concern since the Civil War. A year later came the successful première of *En la ardiente oscuridad* (*In the Burning Darkness*), a metaphysical tragedy depicting students in a school for the blind, written in 1946. This was actually the first play Buero wrote. Buero and some of his critics prefer it over *Story of a Stairway*. The work certainly contains much of the thematics and symbolism which will be more fully developed in his later works.

When Buero won the Lope de Vega Prize, he was virtually unknown. Marqueríe states, in his prologue, that "months, days, hours before these prizes and the première of *Story of a Stairway,* no one or almost no one knew the tall and slender youth who was shy and pale, but who tread firmly and expressed himself softly but precisely and meticulously." The fact that Buero was a novice in the theatrical world and a recent prisoner, as well, gave rise to hostility on the part of some critics, who arbitrarily attacked his plays as overly "pessimistic" and as "fatalistic." He has experienced difficulties in getting some plays approved by the censors, especially those to which political significance may be attributed—notably *Aventura en lo gris* (*Adventure in Grey*), an allegory of the Spanish Civil War written as early as 1949 but not performed until 1963, and *La doble historia del doctor Valmy* (*The Double Case History of Doctor Valmy*), a study of the results of police torture, which was finally premièred at the Gateway Theatre in Chester, England, in an English version, but which as yet has not been performed or even published in Spain.

Despite these continuing problems, however, Buero, without compromising his work ideologically or otherwise, has had performed in Spain some sixteen dramas, including his most recent work, *El sueño de la razón* (*The Sleep of Reason*), a historical recreation of Goya which premièred February 7, 1970, at the Reina Victoria Theater after many problems with censorship. Although Buero has not submitted his plays to competitions after winning the Lope de Vega Prize, many have received, after their première, awards which are granted automatically. The premières of Buero's plays are always eagerly awaited and many become the subject of violent polemics in the Spanish press— proof of their inherent merit. Several of his plays have been performed and published, in translation, in Germany, Italy, France, Portugal, Holland, Norway, Hungary, and Yugoslavia, and in the United States (by university theaters) and Japan, as well.

In 1966, as the result of efforts by several American professors— Robert Kirsner, William McKnight, Anthony Pasquariello, and the late Juan Rodríguez Castellano—Buero was nominated by the United States Embassy in Madrid to be a participant in the International Visitors Program and invited here by the Bureau of Educational and Cultural Affairs of the U.S. Department of State. He lectured at major universities from coast to coast, including North Carolina, Pennsylvania State, New York State at Albany, Columbia, Wisconsin, Illinois, Indiana, Stanford, California at Berkeley and Miami. Papers which Buero gave include "El problema de la esperanza trágica" ("The Problem of Tragic Hope"), "Valle-Inclán y el punto de vista del dramaturgo" ("Valle-Inclán and the Point of View of the Dramatist")—a more extensive version of which was subsequently published in *Revista de Occidente*—and "¿Cómo era Velázquez?" ("What was Velázquez Really Like?"). The interest in the dramatist was so great that he was unable to visit many institutions which extended him invitations.

Buero returned to the United States four years later, in 1970, with his wife, the actress Victoria Rodríguez, who has performed in several of his plays and who won the National Award for Dramatic Interpretation in 1958. Both were guests of honor at a Symposium on the Spanish Theater sponsored by the University of North Carolina at Chapel Hill and Buero addressed the gathering on "Un autor español ante las últimas corrientes escénicas" ("A Spanish Author's Views of the Most Recent Dramatic Trends").

Buero Vallejo is now recognized as Spain's foremost dramatist and his importance to Spanish letters is evinced by his recent election to the Spanish Royal Academy to fill the seat left vacant by the death of Antonio Rodríguez Moñino. The dramatist did not seek the honor. Nevertheless, he was gratified to learn that, although his candidacy was sponsored by the liberal sector of the body, he was elected unanimously, with even the more conservative members voting affirmatively. The respected title may afford him a certain measure of protection from the dangers faced by writers in present-day Spain. He fully intends to accept the responsibilities of the position by attending regularly the sessions of the body.[10]

Today Buero lives and works with his wife and two young sons, Carlos and Enrique, in his apartment on Hermanos Miralles, in a modest section of Madrid. A man of unusual culture, Buero reveals in interviews that he usually spends several hours a day reading—much more time than he devotes to writing. He mentions such authors as Galdós, members of the Generation of '98, Dostoevski, and Kafka—although, at times, he says, he would not put down a book of popular physics for a play.[11] Buero's preferences in the theater run to O'Neill, whom he especially admires and whom he considers the United States's greatest playwright, Shaw, Brecht, Ionesco, and Beckett. As writers who have exerted an acknowledged influence upon his own theater, however, he usually cites authors who are Spanish—Cervantes, Calderón, Unamuno, Galdós—with the sole addition of Ibsen. "Rarely," he states, "is Cervantes mentioned in connection with my work. I consider myself a direct, although very modest, descendent of his. Galdós has influenced me through his novels, not his theater. All the Generation of '98, thinkers and creators."[12] In an interesting conversation with Fernández Cuenca, in *Correo Literario,* he explains his process in writing a play. After evolving, over a period of time, a mental plan for a drama, he briefly outlines, on a piece of paper, each act—characters, situations, and dramatic effects—then for two or three months, he spends his afternoons, and, if necessary, nights, slowly and meticulously writing the work by hand. Later it undergoes revisions which may continue until the evening of the première.[13]

The qualities most often spoken of by critics of Buero's theater are its dignity, nobility, and sincerity. The playwright has remained true to the original aim stated, in 1951, near the beginning of his dramatic career: "Let us cultivate a sincere theater where life—our anxieties, pessimism, and, also, our hopes—are revealed without falsification."[14] This seriousness of purpose results from Buero's concept of the theater, which like all forms

of art, he regards as "a sort of intuitive investigation of reality."[15]
One critic states that, for Buero, the theater is not only a "literary
function," but a "psychic imperative"[16]—an authentically personal
inquiry. For Buero, the theater, like life, is an all-embracing
search for truth. His aim, in the words of one critic, is not only
to "entertain or amuse us, to instruct us, or to give witness to a
particular social situation [. . .] he attempts to inquire into the
social and human reality of our time and of our Spain."[17]

CHAPTER 2

Buero's Ideas on the Theater

> "The rejection of tragedy is nothing but the incapacity to remain hopeful in the face of the total spectacle of life and its defeats."
> —Buero, "Commentary," *Hoy es Fiesta*
> (*Today is a Holiday*)[1]

BUERO Vallejo's theater represents, as we have just seen, a quest for understanding about man and the universe. This quest, according to the dramatist, if it is to reach any profundity, must necessarily take place within the framework of tragedy: "It is tragedy which truly tests man and gives us his total measure: his misery, but, also, his grandeur. To attempt to know man, to simply inquire about him ignoring his tragic situation is an incomplete, illusory, and blind act [...]. Only when the exploration of human problematics has its tragic aspects is it truthful and honest, as well as courageous."[2] In numerous essays Buero has expressed his ideas on the theater and, particularly, on tragedy.

I *Catharsis*

Rejecting prescriptive considerations, Buero is concerned primarily with the "sense" or "spirit" of a literary work rather than its form. It is in this broad and universal sense that he employs the word "tragedy" or "the tragic" in reference to his own plays. To define this "tragic sense" is the purpose of much of Buero's writing.

Many authors maintain that modern science has nullified the idea of self-determination and that, consequently, tragedy is impossible in our day in view of the destruction of man's nobility and dignity. In effect, they reject the idea of catharsis, that is, the purification of the emotions brought about by tragedy. Buero Vallejo, on the other hand, whose plays postulate free

21

will, finds in catharsis the ultimate justification for his theater. He interprets this term as much more than simply a pacification or dissolution of the pity and fear felt by the spectator of a tragedy. Catharsis is, according to his point of view, the transformation or elevation of these emotions from a primitive to a moral or ethical plane. Buero's own tragedies aim to "move the spectator and move him deeply, to confront him with his personal capacity—sometimes so limited!—for becoming cordially interested in human sorrow."[3] In other words, Buero believes that tragedy is an experience that ennobles the individual.

Thus it is that a spectator, after witnessing the performance of a tragic work which deals with human injustices, may be so affected that he leaves the theater with a strong desire to ameliorate the condition of his fellowman. An interesting example of a concrete action of cathartic origin which Buero cites concerns Ehrlich, the discoverer of the cure for syphilis. It was after seeing a performance of Ibsen's *Ghosts*, that he decided to dedicate his life to conquering the disease.[4]

Obviously, tragedy for Buero Vallejo has as an important aim a positive transformation of society. The desire for action which a tragedy may bring about, however, Buero believes, must come "not through explicit considerations or moralization [...] but through the exemplary force of the action and the passions it arouses," that is, "directly through an aesthetic, rather than discursive, impression, for aesthetic beauty is a supreme discovery of man which, by its mere presence, can express everything without saying anything."[5] After this aesthetic beauty, our actions cannot be commonplace. The purpose of tragedy is not to advocate particular social or political action, but to help the spectator feel more deeply the radical problem of man and his destiny. Many modern tragedies tend to be expositions of the evils and injustices of society. However, if the desire for action which a play produces is politically programmatic rather than aesthetically cathartic, Buero would say that it is not a tragedy but a propaganda play.

II   *Tragic Destiny*

Buero Vallejo holds the opinion that the aesthetic is not divorced from the ethical or moral in tragedy. Disagreeing with

Schopenhauer, Buero Vallejo maintains that tragic destiny is not something irrational or arbitrary, but to a large extent the creation of man himself. Fear at the apparent caprice of the gods, in Greek theater, or fear at the apparent meaninglessness or absurdity of the world, in modern theater, Buero believes, are but conceptual and emotive substrata of tragedy. Tragedy tries to show that catastrophe is the consequence of man's errors, of his violation of moral order. Man was always free to choose: in Greek tragedy, the oracles, rather than determining his choice, merely indicated the consequences. Ibsen's *Ghosts* attempts to show that the son's illness results from the excesses of his father and the blind incomprehension of his mother. The tragedy thus deals with the reason for suffering and its relationship to moral responsibility. Buero's own plays underscore this element of human responsibility. The universe imposes limitations, but it is the individual's own moral blindness—his self-deception or unwillingness to confront the reality of his situation, as well as his innate egoism—which prevent him from overcoming these limitations and which bring down upon him suffering and grief.

Buero Vallejo points out, however, that the relation between cause and effect may not always appear to be one of error and punishment. Does Prometheus do wrong in giving fire to man in order to improve the wretched lot of humanity, and is his harsh fate justified? The relationship between "liberty" and "destiny" is complex. Our limited comprehension may make it appear that what is just is unjust. Ultimately, therefore, tragedy must result in an act of faith: "the ultimate and greatest moral effect of tragedy is an act of faith. It consists in leading us to believe that the catastrophe is justified and has meaning, although we may not be able to see its justification or understand that meaning."[6] In tragedy, the absurdity of the world is more a possibility to be investigated than a conclusion to be drawn. This belief that tragedy postulates the existence of justice, meaning, or order in the universe obviously differentiates Buero Vallejo from such existentialist writers as Sartre and Camus.

If tragic destiny, according to Buero Vallejo, is not unjust, neither is it always unfavorable. Buero Vallejo, who is concerned primarily with the sense or spirit of a literary work rather than with prescriptive considerations, defines tragedy as a conflict

between "liberty" (free will) and "necessity" (human limitations).[7] His protagonists struggle against the limitations imposed
by their own moral blindness and incomprehension; in his social
tragedies such as *Las Meninas* (*The Ladies-in-Waiting*), against
the limitations imposed by the egoism and injustice of society;
or, in his metaphysical tragedies such as *En la ardiente oscuridad* (*In the Burning Darkness*), against the limitations imposed
by the Absolute. This struggle between freedom and necessity
which tragedy depicts, however, does not end necessarily with
the victory of the latter. Adverse destiny is a grave probability
of man, but not an intrinsic condition of being human. As proof
of the possible triumph of man's liberty over his limitations,
Buero Vallejo points to such well-known tragedies as *The Eumenides, Iphigenia in Tauris, Oedipus at Colonus, Ajax,* Shakespeare's
Measure for Measure, and O'Neill's *Lazarus Laughed,* which
have conciliatory or even happy endings. These works belie the
inexorable character of adverse Destiny often attributed to
tragedy.[8] Furthermore, in his *Poetics,* Aristotle never says that
an unhappy ending is a requirement of tragedy.

A tragedy may end in the spiritual elevation of the protagonists
who undergo catharsis in their poetic world. This, in turn, brings
about a perception, understanding, or "spiritual awakening,"
which the American dramatist Maxwell Anderson considers the
very essence of tragedy. Buero Vallejo points out that this
awakening may lead to calmness, serenity, and even joy on the
part of the defeated protagonists, as in *Strange Interlude* and
Lazarus Laughed of Eugene O'Neill—indeed, all of O'Neill's
plays are perhaps closer in spirit to Greek tragedy than those of
any other modern dramatist. In both we see the protagonists'
positive acceptance of their fate—proof of what O'Neill has
called the "transfiguring nobility" of tragedy. In *Lazarus Laughed*
this acceptance approaches even exultation and ecstasy, as the
dying protagonist shouts from the flames an enthusiastic "yes."
We see a positive acceptance of fate in many of Buero Vallejo's
own protagonists, who, although they go down to external defeat,
win a sort of interior triumph.

Tragedy, however, may not end only in spiritual sublimation,
but also in actual victory over destiny, that is, in a triumph
which is both internal and external. Buero Vallejo points to the
Greek trilogies or tragic cycles, in which the concatenation of

catastrophies brought about by the error of an ancestor of the hero is broken when the latter, ennobled by suffering and catharsis, comes to believe in his ability to rectify the situation and to trust in the help of the gods who are perforce moved by sincere faith. In consonance with Hegel's emphasis on tragic reconciliation, Buero Vallejo notes that the Orestes cycle ends with the hero's release from punishment for matricide when, deciding not to accept his punishment as inevitable, he seeks the intervention of Pallas and the vengeful Furies are transformed into providential Eumenides.[9] " 'Durch Leiden Freude,' 'through sorrow to joy,' " Buero quotes Beethoven, "This is the ultimate meaning of the tragic."[10] "Even the tragedy which is seemingly most desperate," he states, "is based upon hope and postulates, either explicitly or implicitly, those final Eumenides which every tragic conflict, in its tension, seeks."[11]

Critics have commented on the great beauty of the resolution of *Oedipus at Colonus*. The hero purges himself of his sins of patricide and incest by putting out his eyes, abdicating his throne, and exiling himself from Thebes. For years he wanders about, blind and defenseless. Finally, however, the gods summon him to their midst and, in addition to restoring his eyesight, endow him with supernatural vision—the truth he once erroneously thought was his. "The meaning of tragedy, therefore, is not desperate and closed," Buero points out, "even though it may describe desperations and situations without exit, but the putting forth of a conflict between necessity and liberty, which is often terrible but which, in fact, may be resolved in favor of the latter."[12] For Buero Vallejo, tragedy is always positive. It is an expression of "man's urge to free himself from the bonds—external or internal, social or individual—which enslave him."[13]

III *Optimism and Pessimism*

Nietzsche to the contrary, Buero Vallejo believes that tragedy is the very opposite of pessimism. The sorrow portrayed in tragedy does not necessarily signify pessimism any more than the laughter in comedy necessarily signifies optimism. Important bases of Greek tragedy, Buero points out, were "joy" and "hope" in the "resurrection of Dionysus." Nor can modern tragedy be considered pessimistic, even when the author so intends, for behind his pessimistic philosophy, "there continue to operate, although under very different names, Dionysus and his possible —or certain—resurrection. Authentic pessimism is the opposite of tragedy. Pessimism denies all, but tragedy proposes all types of values."[14] It represents, for Buero Vallejo, an heroic act through which man attempts to understand grief without resigning himself to the idea that it and the world are arbitrary. Tragedy, with the suffering and grief it portrays, is authentically pessimistic only to those who would avoid the problems of their existence. It is gloomy and depressing only to those who are truly depressed.[15]

For Buero Vallejo it is the theater of evasion, rather than tragedy, which patently manifests an inherent pessimism—even though this pessimism may be disguised as laughter and diversion—for in its flight from reality it denies life's meaning.[16] In tragedy, on the other hand, there is only a "provisional pessimism": for tragedy accepts not only the brighter but the darker side of life and on the basis of that acceptance invites us to deduce a positive attitude toward our problems.[17] Tragedy, in short, Buero states, proposes the only genuine optimism possible, that based upon truth.

If tragedy, according to Buero Vallejo, cannot be called pessimistic just because it portrays suffering and anguish, neither can tragedy be so termed because it offers no solutions. Tragedy may suggest or imply ultimate truths or mysteries. However, art is more a matter of implication than explication and should involve the spectator in "active contemplation." If a work does not suggest much more than it explicitly states, it is dead, Buero states.[18] Therefore tragedy does not usually offer explicit answers, either social or transcendental, to the questions which it raises:[19] "A play is not a treatise or even an essay; its mission is to reflect life, and life is usually stronger than ideas. A play which can be advantageously supplanted by an explication of its content is a bad play."[20] Tragedy, indeed, often deals with problems about which we do not have the ultimate knowledge. It must approximate what man intuits of the world's complex and mysterious moral order. Tragedy is a living work of art because it accepts the unfathomable occurrences of the universe and makes man aware of its enormous transcendence. By showing the problems of man and his destiny in all their complexity, the writer of tragedy attempts to arouse man to think.[21]

Buero states that any answers arrived at in his own theater—which is characterized more by "search" than by "affirmation"—[22] are always partial and insufficient. His plays do not imply, generally, "any answer other than the need to continue questioning. And if, in spite of everything, he continues to write, it is in the hope that, in this way, the questions will become more imperative and clear."[23] This questioning, nevertheless, does not exclude the possibility of the existence of positive convictions and definite positions on the part of the author and his works. Buero believes that a great tragic writer—like Unamuno—[24] is one who "has the ability to make us relive the problematical nature of beliefs, no matter how firmly they appear to be held. If this is true, we must understand that he always existentializes to some degree the panorama of human life."[25] Authentic drama, even if it corresponds to a definite ideology, will evince a certain existential problematic. The virtue of existentialism has been, Buero states, precisely this: "to reveal to us, again, the radical character of human life as conflict, as anguish, as intuition, as a problem whose solution cannot be fully attained."[26] It is interesting to note that in this interview Buero characterizes himself as a man of constant philosophical disquiet. He does not adhere rigidly to a definite philosophical system, although he tends toward a very personal type of existentialism, which, we shall see, is, in some respects, akin to that of Unamuno. He also mentions the influence of Kant.

Buero Vallejo's own works are exploratory rather than ideological. The critic Robert Brustein has stated that if plays suffer a treatment that is excessively didactic and express rationalized generalizations based on the playwright's political or sociological doctrines, they are less works of art than "political acts or social gestures."[27] Such plays, Buero states, would be sociology or political science but not social or political theater.[28] Rather than conform to some abstract set of principles imposed from the outside, plays should tell the truth in their own terms. "The basic commitment of art," Buero insists, "is the search for sincerity and truth."[29] It is obvious that if tragedy represents a quest for truth, this truth must be that which comes as the result of this quest. Buero Vallejo asks: "Should the theater stick to the

rational explication of provisional knowledge proceeding from
other fields, or should it venture its own—and since it is intuitive,
often obscure—inquiry into the conflicts which it studies and
imagines? If it is a vehicle of perception and of transformation,
its intrinsic right to explore by suitable means cannot be denied."[30]
    It is evident, thus, that Buero Vallejo is opposed to the ideas
of Brecht, who, rejecting cathartic emotional effects, defends a
theater of alienation, preaching, and persuasion, and denies that
the theater can be a vehicle of perception which depends upon
intuitions which cannot be rationalized. However, Buero points
out that Brecht's best works—*Mother Courage*, *Galileo*, and *The
Caucasian Chalk Circle*—are precisely those in which, his theories
to the contrary, there is a binding emotion capable of affecting
even his ideological adversaries and without which, Buero states,
"there is no great theater from Aeschylus to Miller, from Aeschylus to Brecht himself."[31] Between the didactic, based on the
supposedly rationalized portion of reality, and the poetic, Buero
believes, there must be a delicate balance: "If the poetic is authentic, it weighs so lightly that it will not take much of the didactic
to tip the scales."[32] Although Buero emphasizes the former, he
by no means rejects the latter: "From the time of the Greeks,
the theater has aroused communicative emotions and has made
the spectator identify with the action of the play. From the
Greeks, the theater has prompted critical reflection and alienation of he spectator from the action of the play. To favor one or
the other of these two aspects is to see only one face of dramatic
art."[33] Valle-Inclán's *esperpentos* are good, Buero points out,
precisely because they are not absolute. The former's plays,
like Brecht's, are more complex than his theories of distancing
and alienation. Buero demonstrates that Valle-Inclán at times
looks upon his creatures—including children, who are often
innocent victims—not with the gaze of a demigod, from "on
high," but with a humanizing compassion which makes his
plays not mere farces, but tragic visions of reality in which
there is more of Velázquez than of Goya.[34]
    In short, Buero believes that the purpose of theater—which
is to agitate and disturb, to make man think—is accomplished
more through pathetic than dialectic means. He usually leaves
the ideological conflicts, in his own plays, as unanswered questions. The fact that tragedy often provides no answers does not

mean that it is not optimistic; for tragedy, according to Buero
Vallejo's concept, is founded not on concrete affirmations, but
on the psychological reality of hope.

IV *Hope*

Buero Vallejo has stated that the essence of all tragedy is
probably hope and that this is present even in the apparently
most unpromising situations. This tragic hope is, for him, all-
embracing. In general, however, it has two aspects, which are
never mutually exclusive: hope in an earthly solution to human
problems and hope in some sort of transcendent order in the
universe. Buero Vallejo, like Unamuno, envisions hope as a
constant in man's life. Tragedy reflects the human condition: an
eternal struggle between faith and doubt, with the continuing
accompaniment of hope.[35] Man always hopes. When he feels
despair or agony, he projects, as it were, the reverse side of the
coin of hope, which insists on maintaining its force within his
heart. Without light, there is no darkness; without good, no evil.
Thus, without hope there is no despair or existential anguish.
At most, man may deny life, but his bitter negation occurs within
the framework of his unfulfilled and existing hope. And, even
then, he hopes for something—apart from the tenacious persistence of those hopes which have been defrauded—at the very
least, for a change.

To portray this hope, which embraces both faith and doubt,
then, is one of the major purposes of tragedy: "One hopes. One
always hopes. One hopes without believing in the reality of what
is hoped for. One hopes because it is a tension of man, independent of the rational probability of realizing it. To present
this tension as such, with its probability, but also its improba-
bility, of realization would seem to be the basic objective of
tragedy."[36] Through the cathartic effect of tragedy, this tension
may be resolved, according to Buero, into the calmness and
serenity which we sometimes experience "when we succeed in
glimpsing the secret unity of these seemingly disparate con-
cepts [. . .] when we perceive [. . .] that despair and hope are only
degrees or opposite sides of something great and unchangeable
which lies beyond tragedy but which, only through it, can be
reached."[37] Many of Buero Vallejo's own anguished protagonists

are men of hope, who struggle between doubt and faith, torn between their limitations and their longings, between reality and dreams. Moreover, we shall see that in two of Buero Vallejo's tragedies—*La señal que se espera* (*The Awaited Sign*) and *Hoy es fiesta* (*Today's a Holiday*)—hope forms the major theme.

If tragedy is founded largely on the psychological reality of hope, this means that the ultimate attitude of the writer toward his characters' problems—toward their hopes and their despair—must always be one of hope. Real pessimism, a complete lack of hope, would be so depressing and paralyzing that he would be unable to create. An author always writes out of the indestructible background of a threatened but existing hope. If his hope were completely dead, his anguish would be so great as to make his efforts to create seem useless. The act of writing a tragedy is then, in itself, an act of hope: "The human capacity to resist the most unfortunate reverses and even to triumph over them can hardly be denied, and tragedy helps us to discern this. This ultimate faith pulsates behind all the doubts and failures which are shown on stage. This hope moves the pens which describe the most desperate situations."[38] With respect to his personal faith, Buero explains in a recent statement: "I have, in spite of everything, faith in man, but it is a very cautious faith, faith in the possibility that human history has a trajectory, a meaning, but it is a faith which is guarded and which does not exclude the worst possibilities."[39]

We have previously noted that Buero Vallejo is convinced that an essential function of tragedy is to raise questions which may not be resolved. Even when the author ostensibly provides solutions to problems, he is less concerned with these solutions than he is with the depiction of the human condition, the eternal struggle between faith and doubt—a struggle from which springs the revitalization of all faith, its restatement in man's soul as a "living conflict" rather than a "dead formula."[40] The playwright's firmest convictions necessarily acquire a problematical character as he is forced to rethink and to relive ultimate questions. Tragedy is, then, an expression of faith which doubts: "In his works, the writer of tragedy sets forth, before the world, his burning question, and hopes, from the depths of his heart, that the answer will be a resounding 'yes.' He raises, again and again, the question of the enigma of the world and its grief, precisely because he believes it an enigma—a cipher possessed of meaning—and not a bitter fortuity."[41]

Buero Vallejo conceives of all tragedy as lying between two extreme points or limits: absolute doubt and absolute faith. Some tragedies end in conciliation and harmony, while others end in catastrophe. Some suggest certain truths, as does the Orestes trilogy, while others make negations. The first plays are very near the affirmative paint of faith, that is, of hope fulfilled. The second plays are very close to the opposite point of doubt. Tragedy, however, can move no further in this direction, only toward the affirmative point. For absolute negation, like absolute faith, would destroy tragedy. From one point to the other there is only one pathway, that of hope.[42] Aeschylus' tragedies, Buero says, are so near the affirmative point that they could go no further without falling outside the limits of tragedy which presupposes some degree of doubt or anguish. Euripides' tragedies are so near the point of doubt that they could not go any further without becoming completely pessimistic and therefore no longer tragic. According to Buero, tragedy, from its beginning to the present, from Aeschylus to Sartre and the existentialists, follows the same trajectory of faith in Aeschylus to doubt in Euripides.[43] Most of Buero Vallejo's own tragedies lie somewhere between these two poles, ending ambiguously with a question.

Buero Vallejo's concept of the area of tragedy as a scale with varying degrees of faith and doubt is similar to the concept of the critic Louis Martz, who describes it as a spectrum ranging between the poles of "fruitless suffering" and a "secret cause" which affirms the existence of a universal order. Between these two poles would lie works illustrating varying degrees of doubt and affirmation. Near the negative pole would be the plays of Ibsen and *Othello*; in the middle, *Hamlet* and *Oedipus Rex*; and near the opposite pole *Samson Agonistes* and *Murder in the Cathedral*.[44]

The location of a tragedy on the scale determines its degree of hope or the degree to which faith and doubt vie with each other. But, for Buero Vallejo, hope, to some extent, is always present because it is the *sine qua non* of tragedy. In a tragedy which lies near the point of faith, there is still the hope which postulated the affirmation which the tragedy makes; in a tragedy

which lies very near the point of doubt and which depicts human
destiny as meaningless, there is the hope which, even though it
may be philosophically denied, motivated the writing of the
tragedy.[45] In short, Buero maintains that tragedy is always a
radically hopeful phenomenon.

The effect of tragedy upon the spectator, moreover, is always
to orient him toward hope even though it may appear to invite
him to despair. Ibsen's A Doll's House, Buero remarks, concludes
with an explicit incitement to hope—the hope that Nora and
Helmer may somehow, even if through a miracle, change in such
a way that they may create a true marriage. However, even a
tragedy such as Ghosts, which ends in catastrophe, is an invitation to hope, for by revealing the dangers which beset man,
it invites him to create conditions to prevent future problems.[46]
Buero considers that even works, such as those of Sartre and
Beckett, which depict desperate and closed situations are, like
Ghosts, ultimately "open," for there exists, even if externally
or not within the context of the dramas themselves, the implicit
possibility of a posterior hope. After the spectator confronts the
truth revealed in, and the suffering imposed by, the tragedy, the
ground is cleared for reflections of a positive nature. Catharsis,
as Buero understands it, is precisely this: "that movement or
internal renovation which the spectator undergoes with regard to
the most lucid restoration of his hope."[47]

Buero believes that a rehabilitation of tragedy in Spain is
highly appropriate to the present anguished time—which, he
says, is as tragic as any other, and in consequence, as hopeful.
The Greeks, he indicates, created tragedy precisely when they
began to question and to doubt the infallible force of destiny—
additional proof that tragedy does not signify true pessimism.
"A tragic theater," Buero states, "has always been the best
measure of a people's vitality and courage in the face of their
destiny."[48]

V Form

We have seen that, in keeping with vital rather than prescriptive considerations, Buero considers tragedy a flexible literary tendency determined more by feeling than by form. In
this sense, the tragic has not been lacking in Spanish theater.

Buero points to Calderón's *La vida es sueño* (*Life is a Dream*), which departs from the existential and typically tragic considera- tion that "man's greatest sin is to have been born"—so frighten- ing, Buero remarks, to those for whom religion is a consolation which comforts rather than a conflict which challenges. Based on the supposed fatidic power of an omen, the play is a tragedy because of its metaphysical mystery, the moral relationship established between Segismundo's actions and their conse- quences, and its cathartic effect upon both protagonist and spec- tator. He points out that the conciliatory ending of Lope de Vega's *Fuenteovejuna* (*Sheep's Well*) recalls the traditional reconciliations of Greek tragedy. Tragic elements are found, likewise, in such dramas as *El caballero de Olmedo* (*The Knight of Olmedo*), *El médico de su honra* (*The Doctor of his Honor*), and many others beginning, of course, with *La Celestina*, and extending to plays of such modern authors as Galdós, Unamuno, and Lorca.[49]

As we have seen, Buero points out that tragedy may be expressed under diverse forms: tragicomic, novelesque—as is obvious in the case, for example, of *Don Quijote*. He singles out Kafka's *The Castle* as among the greatest tragedies of our own times. Within the theater itself, he believes that the aesthetic or formal differences between ancient and modern tragedy are unimportant, since the problematics are fundamentally the same —God or the gods have been replaced by the Absurd or the imperfection of the social structure. Moreover, such require- ments of classic tragedy as the nobility or elevation of the charac- ters, situations, and language, which have now been aban- doned, were but relative even for the Greeks. Neorealism has employed natural dialogues and humble characters and situa- tions which, through their simplicity and truthfulness, have done much to make tragedy more meaningful to the average man.[50] Nevertheless, the formal differences between classic and mod- ern tragedy, Buero points out, are not as great as commonly believed, as evidenced by the use of the chorus in such modern works as Lorca's *Yerma*, masks in Pirandello's *Six Characters in Search of an Author* and O'Neill's *Lazarus Laughed*, and music in *Peer Gynt* and the dramas of Brecht. Moreover, from the be- ginning of the nineteenth century, European theater has gen- erally followed a "closed" construction, that is to say, a construction which is based, to a large extent, upon the classic unities.[51]

Buero has never denied the validity of any dramatic form, including the "open" or "functional" form characterized by certain cinematographic techniques: numerous short scenes, rapid changes of place, flashbacks, and plastic effects. However, he believes that the new writer should prove himself first by following a "closed form," for the more facile form often disguises the ineptitude of the beginner: "An author should dominate his craft and the cultivation of a closed form is the only way of doing it. No better guarantee than that of his professional honesty."[52] Early in his career, most of Buero's plays were of this "closed" construction and several presented especially challenging technical problems. In *Story of a Stairway,* all of the action takes place, as the title indicates, on the stairway of a tenement house; and, in *Today's a Holiday,* on an apartment house rooftop in the space of one holiday; in *Madrugada (Dawn),* a clock on stage visibly marks the identification of real with theatrical time. In later plays, starting with *Un soñador para un pueblo (A Dreamer for a People)* in 1958, Buero has, due to the historic nature of their content, of necessity employed an "open" or "functional" form although he has avoided a proliferation of scenes destructive of continuity.

Always interested in formal renovation, Buero has been particularly concerned, as far back as his earliest plays, with the problem of audience identification with the dramatic action. He points out that "participation" of the spectator has always been the aim of theater, from the time of its origin with the Greeks, despite current use of the word to describe certain dramatic techniques now in vogue—techniques which evolved as a reaction to the "theater of consumption." The recent "theater of protest," denying that what the spectator wants is necessarily what he needs, has attempted to evolve more authentic "participation," an attempt which, as we shall see, Buero does not believe has been successful.[53]

The "theater of participation" is often regarded as the opposite of, or an answer to, Brecht and his theories of distancing. Buero points out, however, that the aim of both is the same; for to reflect critically—the result expected from distancing—is, in itself, to "participate." Partisans of the most radical forms of participatory theater invoke as precursors and models the names of Alfred Jarry and Antonin Artaud. The latter attempted to reform the theater, and society, by combating what he regarded as "narrow bourgeois rationality." Abandoning rational devices and discursive thought, Artaud sought to provide in his "theater of cruelty" an intuitive image of what language is incapable of putting into words. Relegating dialogue to the background, he attempted to reveal, through the language of gesture, movement, and action, the obscure and sinister depths of man's mind and his cruel, often enigmatic, instincts. He sought to confront man with his erotic obsessions, his savagery, and even his cannibalism. Brecht, on the other hand, in view of what he considered "bourgeois irrationality," strove to create a reflective scientific theater. Whereas Artaud proclaimed the necessity for a return to primitive myth and magic, Brecht preached the destruction of all myth. However, both dramatists, seemingly opposed, looked for a new type of participation: the spectator's reencounter with his own authenticity and, consequently, his communicative participation in the dramatic action. Both theatrical tendencies, seemingly irreconcilable, are linked by their desire for renovation and revolution, both in the theater and in society—to such a degree that significant dramatists have attempted to integrate them. Buero singles out three leading dramatists of the German-speaking world today: Friedrich Dürrenmatt, Peter Weiss, and Max Frisch, who have injected into the reflexive distancing of the Brechtian tradition—their point of departure—emotive participation and the surprise occasioned by the irrational. Buero's own plays, as we shall see, often incorporate these two elements, both of which, he believes, are fundamental to good theater.[54]

Recently, however, Buero finds that this equilibrium between communicative emotion and identification characteristic of Artaud, who attempts to disclose the obscure, enigmatic depths of man, and the critical reflection and alienation advocated by Brecht has been threatened by the increasing influence, especially in the United States, of the youth protest movement upon theatrical groups who share their vision of a radical transformation of society: the Living Theater of Julian Beck and Judith Malina, the Bread and Puppet Theater of Peter Schumann, a street theater group from New York, and others such as Roy Hart's. Finding their inspiration in Artaud, these groups seek desperately to force the spectator to "participate" in a physical manner. Not content with a psychic participation or reflection which permits the spectator to remain in his seat, they attempt to make him into an active creative protagonist in the dramatic action— just as youth protest, Buero notes, seeks to convert the public, and not merely leaders, into protagonists of history. The actors mingle among the audience and, by either friendly invitation or insult and provocation, seek to convert the spectator into an active participant rather than a passive "consumer," to make him improvise, enter into a "happening" upon stage in which he sings and dances along with the actors, or, if he prefers, to leave the theater—anything so long as he "acts."[55]

In recent lectures at the University of North Carolina and at the Annual World Congress of Authors in Las Palmas, Buero maintains that this type of invitation may not produce the desired result. Present-day society, faced with the necessity of a profound and perhaps painful transformation toward something they cannot foretell and hence is terrifying, feels a tremendous disconcertation which often makes attempts at social participation and renovation assume a tragic character. In a world in which participation in life is difficult, the desperate insistence upon a crassly physical—not only psychic—participation is understandable, Bureo believes, but counterproductive in that it is inhibiting to a large sector of the audience. Buero distinguishes between three groups of spectators. One group, repulsed by what they see on stage, leaves the theater. Some do participate physically, albeit, Buero believes, superficially. However there are many, Bureo states, like himself, who, although they want to collaborate with the actors, feel themselves outside of, rather than inside of, the action. The spectator is more likely to be convinced, Buero believes, by the imperceptible force, emotion, or lucidity of the performance than by a direct, often brusque and aggressive exhortation to action which he may automatically react against. The intelligent person, moreover, may sense the element of falsity and blind mimicry inherent in this type of theater. Buero notes, for example, that, at the performance of *Hair* which he attended in London, the almost orgiastic "happening" at the end when some of the audience joined the actors on stage to dance to the accompaniment of "pop" music ended abruptly after fifteen minutes when a bell rang—which would not have happened if the orgy had been real. In the latter case, it would have given rise, perhaps, to things which we should not prefer to see on stage, but which would, at least, have been authentic.[56]

In *The Birth of Tragedy*, Nietzsche describes the two fundamental impulses of tragedy as the lucent, measured or ordered "Apollonian," and the dark, sensuous, frenzied, and orgiastic "Dionysian." Buero finds that, at first glance, the emphasis on physical participation in today's theater would seem to represent an increase in the "Dionysian"—a phenomenon paralleled outside the theater by the style of faunlike long hair, youth protest, the rupture with convention, etc. Buero points out that for the "Dionysian" to be authentic—serious and salutary or beneficial—it must be balanced by the "Apollonian." However, the perfect blending of these two motives found in Greek culture has now been lost. This explains, Buero believes, why the current theater, which accentuates the "Dionysian" as a form of rupture with the lies and hypocrisy of society, leads not to true liberation or inner freedom, but to what he considers an accelerated form of neurosis.[57]

Buero notes that his own reservations concerning what he considers the excesses of such groups as the Living Theater—the trend toward the atextual productions advocated by Artaud and toward extreme forms of participation—are shared by such widely differing directors as Jorge Lavelli and Roger Planchon in France and by director Peter Brook in England.[58] It is for this reason he believes possible a new reconciliation between participation and distancing, between the "Dionysian" and "Apollonian," which will represent a return to true tragedy as he has so often defined it and which we attempted to describe above. In their desperation disguised as joy, today's radical playwrights wish to erase theatrical history and return not to tragedy, but to the dithyramb, which was its origin, with its spontaneous chorus of spectator-actors as protagonist. If theater is to return to tragedy, which went beyond the dithyramb to give us man's total measure—his lucidity as well as his enigma—Buero believes that it must result from the realization that authentic participation in the theater, like authentic action in life, must be internal as well as external.[59]

The psychic participation which Buero advocates is best

illustrated by two of his own plays. In one of his very earliest plays, *In the Burning Darkness*, the characters are blind. Instead of having the actors approach the spectators to shout at them the horrors of blindness or forcibly to blindfold them, he extinguishes, at one point, both the stage and house lights. That this participation, although less ostensible, was effective was proved by the screams of the audience. In a very recent work, *El sueño de la razón* (*The Sleep of Reason*), the protagonist is deaf. Rather than the actors violently covering the spectators' ears and then screaming at them, they move their lips but utter no sound whenever the protagonist is on stage, thus permitting the audience to enter into his world of deafness. Thus there is produced a more authentic participation in the reality of the tragedy—a reality which is symbolic, for the blindness portrayed represents, as we shall see, man's lack of spiritual vision and the deafness, his alienation or estrangement from his fellow human beings.[60]

Buero rejects such simplistic categorizations as "realistic" and "symbolic." In an exchange between Miguel Luis Rodríguez and Buero published in *Indice*, the former contends that "realistic" dramas are superior to "symbolic" ones because they are more readily understandable by the public and because they reflect to a greater extent the "reality" of our times.[61] For this reason he prefers Buero's so-called "realistic" plays such as *Story of a Stairway* and *Today's a Holiday* over his so-called "symbolic" ones. Buero replies that the mere definition of such terms as "realistic" and "symbolic" is difficult and discusses his own concept of "symbolic realism," using Galdós as an example. This "realistic" novelist, he points out, is a subtle symbolist whose novels are replete with sometimes transcendent and mysterious meaning. Since all art is condensation, Buero states, the most realistic art is also symbolic, for it involves "the implicit, not the explicit meaning of things which, strictly speaking, the anecdote does not contain." Buero believes that a literary work should be symbolic in the same sense that reality itself is. By "symbols" he means not "theorems" or "syllogisms," but "the meanings subtly encompassed by life and by literature which reflects it."[62] Buero points out that "reality" and "realism" are not synonymous and that the former is all-inclusive. He quotes Goethe's dictum: "the opposite of truth to reach the height of reality." Buero believes that great artists counterbalance both realism and symbolism in their works and that it would be difficult to deny symbolic value to the plays cited by Rodríguez as "realistic" (*Death of a Salesman, Strange Interlude, Desire under the Elms*), or the relevance to reality of such "symbolic" works as *The Emperor Jones, No Exit*, or *Waiting for Godot*.[63]

Whereas Rodríguez attacks the historical symbolism of Arthur Miller's *The Crucible*, which deals with the Salem witch hunts, for lessening the "direct reality" of the play, Buero recalls that the Greeks, Shakespeare, and others situated in the past many of their most relevant works. He points out that Brecht, the advocate of a militant "social realism," locates his best plays in a past which is somewhat atemporal and therefore symbolic and does not hesitate to use such expressionistic or indirect techniques as masks, spotlights, etc. Brecht's theory of distancing—with which, as we have seen, Buero is not in total accord—is, indeed, one of "reflective approach to reality by means of a departure from direct realism."[64]

While Rodríguez considers the conclusion of Priestley's *An Inspector Calls* defective because of its "concession to the supernatural," Buero praises it for leaving the problem of the possible "unreality" of the events described—both the girl's death and the visit of the inspector to investigate it—unanswered. Such "unrealities" Buero considers "complexities and subtleties" of a reality which at times may seem clear but often obscure and enigmatical and which reveals constantly changing facets. Buero rejects no literary technique: "I believe that in the literary nothing can be excluded and that direct, psychological, or imaginative realism is appropriate, as is the combination of all these things. I even believe in the legitimacy of allegory. [...] In our epoch all these schools and tendencies have a place and this variety is not a sign of decadence but of vitality."[65] If the mission of art is the aesthetic exploration of reality, Buero believes there is no single way or exclusive manner of achieving this.[66]

CHAPTER 3

Man's Quest for the Impossible Dream

"But for that we need a universal promise, a
bond of love which only women dream of at
times."

—*La tejedora de sueños* (*The Dream
Weaver*)[1]

FOR Buero Vallejo, as we have seen, tragedy, like all art,
represents an intuitive form of perception and exploration of
reality, a search for understanding about man and the world.
This quest for truth which tragedy proposes may take the form
of a search on the part of one or more of the characters, who
embody the preoccupations of the author. Often, although not
always, the characters' search is a conscious one. Some of Buero's
characters search for the understanding or truth which will
permit them to find an earthly solution to human problems;
others, for the truth which will enable them to find a metaphysical justification for the world. Of course, these two searches
for truth usually overlap, for the transcendent is rooted in everyday life.

The knowledge for which Buero's characters search is often
represented by the symbolism of light and darkness, vision and
blindness. It is interesting to note that these symbols are the
same which Sophocles used in his Oedipus plays which depict
the hero's quest for understanding about who he is. Buero
defines "light" in his theater as any sort of comprehension or
"superior illumination, rational or irrational, which can diminish
or overcome our limitations."[2] The other half of the metaphor is
blindness. Blindness, Buero has said, is a lack of vision. To
conquer it is therefore to see or to discover a facet of truth. It is
likewise a limitation to man's freedom, to his free self-develop-
ment, and so represents the core of any tragic problem, which
is always "the struggle of man, with his limitations, for his

40

liberty."[3] This blindness, in Buero's theater, is double: (1) man's blindness to his own nature, which prevents his self-realization as he blames his failures on adverse circumstances instead of his own faults and errors, and (2) man's blindness to metaphysical truth, which prevents his finding meaning in life. The two plays in which this struggle for light is most obvious are *En la ardiente oscuridad* (*In the Burning Darkness*), the first work Buero wrote, and *El concierto de San Ovidio* (*Concert at Saint Ovide*), which is more recent. In these tragedies characters who are physically blind symbolize the problems of man in general. However, these preoccupations are present—either implicitly or explicitly—in all of Buero's theater. "The unifying purpose of all my work," he states, "has surely continued to be the same: that of opening man's eyes."[4]

A major obstacle to solving human problems, in Buero's theater, is man's self-deception, his unwillingness to confront the reality of his situation, to face truths which may be painful but without the acceptance of which there can be no possibility of solutions. A question basic to all of Buero's theater, therefore, is that of escapism versus realism, illusion versus truth. One critic has stated the problem as follows: "Fictitious tranquility or yearning for the infinite? Indifference or agony? Human snail or man of flesh and blood who suffers because he wants to know the secret of his existence?"[5] Buero's answer is to be found in *In the Burning Darkness* when Ignacio says to Carlos, the advocate of a tranquil blindness to life's more profound and tragic aspects: "You have no right to live, because you insist on not suffering, because you refuse to confront your tragedy . . . by trying to forget."[6] The meaning of existence, Buero implies, is found through searching for the truth despite the suffering this implies. Upon the tragic hero, it has been said, "suffering is never merely imposed: he incurs it by his own decision which springs from his desire for the deepest kind of knowledge."[7]

The attitude of Buero is the exact reverse of that of the "theater of evasion." In the latter, the characters escape from the real world, with its anguish and suffering, to a world of pretense, of illusory appearances, of darkness. This world of darkness or blindness is precisely where Buero's tragedies start. The search for "light" in both ancient Greek and modern tragedy is accompanied by anguish; but underlying this anguish is always hope:

hope in man's attaining deeper understanding both of himself and of the universe. Tragedy is a pilgrimage towards truth,
even though the truth to which modern man aspires is usually
tentative and precarious, not the sudden and complete illumination which comes to Oedipus in a blinding flash of light. Tragedy,
Buero believes, "affirms nothing definitive regarding our human
limitations but rather proposes the encounter with those truths,
or, at least, with those searches which can, perhaps, free us from
our blindness."[8]

For convenience of discussion, we divide Buero's tragedies into
two major groups corresponding to what he has pointed out as
the two poles of all theater: (1) the social or vital pole, where the
solution to the problems presented is generally human; and (2)
the metaphysical pole.[9] These two groups are formed by those
plays which deal primarily with the two themes with which,
Buero states, tragedy deals: man's search for the understanding
which may enable him to (1) realize his human potential and (2)
find metaphysical meaning in life.[10] We shall see, however, that
these two searches are almost never mutually exclusive.

In the first group of tragedies dealing with man's struggle for
self-realization are several works which depict the problem
of achieving meaningful human relationships. Buero Vallejo is
concerned with the theme—so important in twentieth-century
theater—of the radical solitude of the individual and his seeming
inability to communicate meaningfully. We see the constant
conflict which seems to characterize human relationships and
the barriers which separate man from his fellow human beings.
Indeed, effective communication or unity with other individuals
often appears virtually unattainable. This lack of comprehension
and communication is often the result of man's spiritual blindness—the egoism which prevents sympathy, compassion, and
charity. Many of Buero's protagonists struggle to free themselves
from their blindness. This search for understanding or "light"
necessarily brings anguish as they force themselves to confront
the insincerity and hypocrisy on which their relationships with
others are often based. Three of Buero's tragedies, however—
Las palabras en la arena (*The Words in the Sand*), 1949, *La
tejedora de sueños* (*The Dream Weaver*), 1952, and *Casi un
cuento de hadas* (*Almost a Fairy Tale*), 1953—depict several

characters who are unwilling to confront the reality of their blind incomprehension, self-deception, and evasion.

The first two tragedies deal with the problems of adultery and marital honor and contrast egoistic love, which is incapable of pardon, with pure unselfish love.

I Las palabras en la arena (The Words in the Sand)

The Words in the Sand is a one-act play based on the incident of the woman caught in adultery (John VIII:1-11), in which Jesus said, "Let him who is without sin among you be the first to cast a stone." In accord with patristic tradition,[11] Buero has Jesus indicate, by writing in the sand, the secret sins of various members of the mob which he is trying to dispel. Among the angriest and most violent of the crowd, in Buero's play, is Asaf, an arrogant young captain in the Sanhedrin Guard. Since he knows himself to be innocent of the sin indicated, Asaf scorns Jesus' words. Buero explains, in a commentary, that he thought it likely that some of the words which Jesus wrote might have referred to future actions and, therefore, have provoked only ridicule on the part of those to whom they referred.[12] Shortly after the incident described above, Asaf learns from an indiscreet servant girl that his wife Noemi has committed adultery with a Roman centurion. After a scream from within the house, he confesses that the word that Jesus wrote in the sand was "murderer."

The contrast between the attitudes of Asaf and of Jesus is seen clearly in the former's words to his wife, whose compassion toward the biblical adulteress he condemns and of whose own infidelity with the centurion he is perhaps only partially unconscious:

ASAF: *(Almost shouting.)* The law of Moses is final!
NOEMI: *(Bitterly.)* You speak like a Pharisee.
ASAF: And you speak just like the Galilean, just like that dangerous agitator, who wants to destroy our homes and to forgive, always to forgive! But if one forgives there can be no family, no loyal wife, no obedient children, no State, nothing! *(He is red in the face.)* (p. 92)

It is in Asaf's arrogance and brutal vindictiveness towards the biblical adulteress that Jesus, with his intuitive understanding of human nature, doubtlessly foresaw his destiny. As we are told by La Fenicia, the servant girl who watches the crowd from the garden wall, it is Asaf who demands the stoning with the greatest vehemence. The role of Jesus' prophecy is thus quite similar to that played by the oracles in Greek tragedy in that it predicts rather than predestines.

Asaf, the protagonist of *The Words in the Sand*, is an excellent sample of the "tranquil blindness,"[13] that is, the insincerity and evasion with which Buero is concerned in his theater. That Asaf is made uneasy by the word of Jesus is obvious in his refusal to tell anyone, including his wife, what the word was which Jesus wrote. To quiet his incipient anxiety, however, he dismisses Jesus as a "dreamer" and his words as "insignificant words in the sand . . . words that the wind erases." Many of his words and actions reveal that he is only partially unconscious of his wife's infidelity and that, in view of his brutal violence, he is capable of becoming sufficiently enraged to kill her.

In his conversation with Noemi we see his vindictiveness toward the adulteress and his suspicion when his wife expresses compassion for her. When, with feigned humility, Noemi then asks him to forgive her, Asaf's enigmatic answer is indicative of his doubts: "Yes, this time. But you will have to pay for your errors." These doubts are also seen in his attitude when she delays outside the house to intercept the servant girl who returns from delivering a message to the Roman centurion. Asaf's suspicion is, indeed, the reason for the intensity of his feelings against the biblical adulteress and for his leadership in the attempt to stone her which prefigures his subsequent murder of Noemi.

Asaf, however, refuses to admit to himself the truth about his wife. Even when he discovers La Fenicia with the bag of money given her by the centurion, he tries to believe, until she informs him otherwise, that it is she who is the guilty one. If Asaf had wanted to learn the truth and had reflected with sincerity, he would easily have seen, in his wife's attitude toward the biblical adulteress, her own infidelity and read in his own brutality and propensity to violence, as did Jesus, an indication of his probable destiny. It is his spiritual blindness, his failure to come to grips with reality, to face the problems of his relationship with his wife and of his own character, to admit to himself, in short, the possibility that Jesus' prophecy might be true, which brings about his downfall.

Buero explains that the play is "not a stone cast at anyone but rather a humble attempt on the part of the author to understand and to help others to understand some of the labyrinths in which man's morality is lost."[14] He believes that adultery is a theme which should be treated with the same dignity in the theater as it is in the Gospel: "For the Gospel is revealing and courageous; it brings human faults out into the open instead of hiding them. It transforms them into exemplary written meditations, not taboos."[15]

The play thus emphasizes the need for conjugal trust and understanding. The hatred and vindictiveness of Asaf are contrasted to the compassion and pardon of Jesus, even though the latter never appears on stage. The moral darkness of traditional law codes which demand blood vengeance to satisfy man's egoism is contrasted with the light of the new Christian ethic. Buero remarks that Jesus' words of pardon are "called to imprint for ever, and above the level of the false honor codes which we at times forge, the epithet of 'murderer' on the forehead of him who satisfies his vanity by shedding his wife's blood."[16]

Although the play ends in catastrophe, there remains the hope that the other Jews will profit from Asaf's example. The scribe Eliú, the Sadducee Gadi, the Pharisee Matatías, and the Priest Joazar, all members of the mob that wish to stone the adultress at the beginning of the play, echo Asaf's protests of innocence, but know in their heart that Jesus' words about them—"robber of the poor," "child molester," "hypocrite," and "atheist"—are true. As Asaf emerges from the house to confess his crime. they surround him and begin to question him in a repetition of the choral effect of the opening scene. The tragedy ends as "the servant girl kneels, also, moaning. The rest rise up with frightened eyes, and Destiny rests its trembling gaze upon the ancient group which surrounds the defeated man" (p. 99).

II   La tejedora de sueños (The Dream Weaver)

Like Asaf, Ulises (Ulysses) in *The Dream Weaver,* leads a life of spiritual blindness and hypocrisy. It is his failure to come to grips with the truth about himself which causes his defeat,

just as it causes Asaf's. The protagonist of the play, however,
is Penelope. Termed by Valbuena Prat "perhaps one of the best
examples of the renovation of a mythic theme in our time,"[17]
The Dream Weaver is described by its author as the "interior
tragedy" of a Greek myth. In a commentary Buero explains that
he considers Penelope's problem similar to that of all the Greek
women who were abandoned when their husbands went to Troy.
These women are possible subjects of an inner tragedy far more
profound than the exterior one of Clytemnestra, who took a
lover and with his help murdered her husband.[18] Men start
wars, Penelope tells Ulysses in Buero's play, "in order to make
us suffer the consequences. We want peace, husbands, and
children... and you give us wars, you thrust us into the danger
of adultery and turn our sons into our murderers."[19] Buero states,
in his commentary, that since Penelope was the purest and most
prudent of these women deserted by their husbands, she was,
therefore, perhaps the most tortured. He comments that to show
this "does not imply a strange rejection or destruction, but a
very human and pitying clarification of her suffering figure, whose
ultimate nobility is resplendent throughout the harsh struggle
of her prolonged period of fidelity."[20]

Buero's Penelope no longer weaves dreams of Ulysses, whose
absence is motivated not by patriotism, but lust for Helen, and
whose return is occasioned only by the latter's loss of youth and
beauty. She dreams of Anfino (Amphinomus), the idealistic
young suitor with whom she has fallen in love despite her
external fidelity to her husband. Buero explains that he has
developed certain ideas which he considers implicit in *The
Odyssey*. Buero interprets Ulysses, who disguises himself upon
returning home in order to spy upon his wife, and who kills
all her suitors, as a calculating egoist who knows nothing about
love.[21] He presents him as astute and devious, a "petty reasoner"
in contrast to Anfino, who, like Penelope herself, represents the
idealist, the dreamer.

Penelope's interior tragedy is represented by the secret figures
which she weaves in the small locked room, symbolic of her
soul, figures which portray her solitary dreams and illusions,
her love for Anfino, which she knows can probably never be
fulfilled. Penelope cannot marry Anfino for the other suitors,
who are interested in her wealth, would kill him out of envy.

This she explains to him in the conversation in which she reveals her love. Anfino tells Penelope that there can be only one reason for her unraveling her weaving by night: "I'm a man and I know how to reason things out. [. . .] There's only one explanation. You love Ulysses and mean to wait for him as long as you live" (p. 37). But Penelope answers that she knows that Anfino is the only one of the suitors who loves her and who would be content to live with her in poverty. Moreover, he is the only one who is willing to wait; for only he sees her eternally young. Therefore, she explains, "I decided to let them rob me of everything. That's why I unravel the pattern every night. . . . Widowed, I no longer think of Ulysses . . . because I don't know how to reason" (p. 40). It is now that the significance of the mysterious figures becomes clear: "They're . . . my dreams. Dreams which I must unravel every night in order that, someday, I may make them real" (p. 40).

However, when Ulysses returns home and learns that Penelope has betrayed him (although only in her dreams and without anyone else's knowledge), like the typical Calderonian husband he punishes her by killing Anfino before her very eyes—even though he himself has been guilty of equal or greater infidelity in leaving her for Helen. He then condemns her to a feigned role of exemplary wife, ordering her weavings destroyed and composing a new rhapsody for the slaves to sing about her fidelity:

> Her name, Penelope the Queen
> a model for all wives forever.
> She weaves her household dreams in cloth
> and her modesty shines like a gem . . . (p. 72)

"I am the king of Ithaca," he explains, "our name must remain free of stain and be resplendent for posterity. No one will know of this" (p. 70). Although love may perish, appearances must be maintained. The purpose for which he has returned is to preserve his prestige as king.

To Penelope, the contrast between Ulysses and Anfino is clear. When she has confessed to the latter that she started her weavings only as a revenge against Helen and that she enjoyed the rivalry over her and tried to prolong it out of vanity, Anfino

can forgive her. "You understand it," Penelope tells him, "and
you alone forgive" (p. 165). Anfino, moreover, gives his life
willingly for his love. He alone, out of all the suitors, does not
flee the arrows of Ulysses: "I defended Penelope, Ulysses. But
I accept death at your hand. [...] I thank you for your arrow,
Ulysses. Death is the great dream that frees us.... And my
thanks to you for your dreams, Penelope" (p. 64).

Buero comments that if Ulysses is, for Penelope, "the old
man" in Pauline terminology, Anfino then represents "the new
man." The latter's "practical morality" contrasted to the "cold
and utilitarian political morality" of Ulysses is that of a "pre-
Christian." We thus have the same opposition as in *The Words
in the Sand*: egoistic love which demands vengeance (Asaf's and
Ulysses') and pure unselfish or ideal love which is capable of
understanding and pardon (Jesus' and Anfino's). In both plays
it is spiritual blindness to this higher type of love which causes
the tragedy. When Ulysses declares, at the end, that all is lost
because Penelope still loves Anfino and that the gods have thus
worked their undoing, Penelope responds, "Don't blame the
gods.... We fashion our own downfall" (p. 70).

In the rebellious confrontation—made all the more dramatic
by our awareness of the presence of Anfino's body behind the
balustrade—Penelope points out to Ulysses the reasons for his
failure to maintain her love: his own distrust and suspicion.
Penelope unveils his "prudence" as cowardliness and lack of
faith. Ulysses has disguised himself because he does not dare
to believe in either Penelope or himself, because he fears that
he will find her old and that he himself, with his wrinkles and
white hair, will be unable to please her.

PENELOPE: Now I must tell you that your cowardice has destroyed
     everything. Nothing had happened between Anfino and myself
     before your arrival, do you hear me? Nothing ... except my
     poor dreams as I slept alone. If you had come to me honestly,
     courageously and offered me your gray hairs ennobled by war
     and suffering, perhaps I would have responded in time. In
     spite of everything, you would have been that courageous
     man all women dream of.... The Ulysses I dreamt of during
     those early years.... And not this sly, hypocritical coward
     who comes as a vile old man to destroy all my illusions!
   [...]

That gigantic heart of his which you destroyed loved my youth and my beauty! ... There's only one way you could have beaten him! ... To have had the courage of your feelings as he did; to have come determined to find the gentle and lovely Penelope you left behind. And immediately I would have found in you, once again, the man of my dreams. (p. 70)

Ulysses returns home, in the words of one critic, as "a man devoid of the moral courage to accept the truth of the situation and to reach a deeper understanding with his wife."[22] Now, although he has his wife, he has nothing, only "the appearance, the laughable shell of a marriage."[23] The purely external nature of the victory which Ulysses wins as he destroys Penelope's weavings, is pointed up, at the end, by the ironic song of the chorus praising Penelope's fidelity to her husband. Its words are like the "icy words" of the cynical and rationalistic Ulysses himself. Penelope, like him, goes down to defeat; but she wins what Buero calls, in his commentary, the internal victory; for she will always be young and beautiful in Anfino's dreams: "It's you ... you alone ... who've lost. I've won! [...] You will never have a woman to remember your youth ... for you were born old. But I will always be young. Young and beautiful in Anfino's memory and eternal dreams" (p. 70). From this internal victory springs the infinite hope with which the tragedy ends: Whereas in *The Words in the Sand* hope is only implicit and external to the action of the tragedy, here it is explicit.

PENELOPE: (... *transfigured, with uplifted eyes* ...) ... There are no more figures to weave, and the chamber of my soul is empty. But I still have something ... my Anfino (*with a sob*), Oh, Anfino! Wait for me. Some day I'll go to join you. (p. 72)

Penelope's hope is not limited, however, to another world where Anfino awaits her. For she envisions a day, on earth, when there will be "a universal bond of love," the reflection of the mercy and forgiveness of Anfino and of Jesus:

PENELOPE: (*Intent upon the corpse.*) Wait ... wait for the day when men will be like you ... and not like him. A day when men will have courage and show kindness to everyone. When they will no longer make war or abandon us. Yes ... that day will come [...] when there are no more Helens ... or Ulysses in the

world. But for that we need a universal promise, a bond of
love which only women dream of ... at times. (p. 72)

The tragedy thus ends ambivalently, with a question full of hope.
Many works of modern Spanish literature—Pérez de Ayala's
Tigre Juan (*Tiger Juan*) with its sequel *El curandero de su honra*
(*The Restorer of His Honor*), for example—attempt to illustrate
the Calderonian *pundonor* or point of honor. A very similar
message of tolerance and freedom from old ideas is found in
The Words in the Sand and *The Dream Weaver*. Both plays
seek to show that generosity and human understanding are more
important than the dead letter of so-called honor codes. Both
condemn vengeance, whether employed to satisfy the Hebrew
law of the talion or to preserve royal prestige for reasons of state.

III   Casi un cuento de hadas (Almost a Fairy Tale)

Hope for a very similar "promise" or "bond of love" is represented by Riquet and Leticia in *Almost a Fairy Tale*, a free version of "Riquet à la houppe" ("Riquet of the Tuft"), Perrault's
tale of the ugly but intelligent prince and the beautiful but stupid
princess. In Perrault's story, a fairy predicts, at their births,
that the prince will be able to transmit his intelligence to the
woman he loves and that the princess will have the power to
give her beauty to the one she chooses. The tale's theme, Buero
comments, is the magical power of love to transform, for Perrault
states: "It was not the charm of the fairy but love alone which
accomplished this metamorphosis."[24]

In Buero's tragedy a kindly old woman, a "humanized fairy,"
summons the ugly Riquet to the palace where the lovely but
unhappy princess Leticia is regarded by all as stupid and therefore unmarriageable. By his love and encouragement, Riquet
gradually succeeds in awakening the wit of the princess, who,
formerly intimidated by the lack of affection in the court, now
gains confidence in herself. In turn, the deformed Riquet, with
his unruly red shock of hair, becomes for Leticia "a handsome
prince on whose head the golden tuft glows like a flame" (p. 28).
The ugly prince—whose appearance, it should be noted, is "frightful" but never "ridiculous," and whose expression is intelligent
and noble—and the handsome prince whom Leticia sometimes

succeeds in seeing are actually played by different actors. The appearance of the ugly, and of the handsome Riquet into whom he is sometimes transformed, is often accompanied by soft violin music—appropriate to the eighteenth-century, fairy tale palace in which Buero sets the action. This music, which Buero suggests may be Handel's "Water Music," represents, in the words of one critic, "the illusion of his beauty when seen through the eyes of love."[25]

"Love," says Riquet, "enlivens the spirit of the beloved and also embellishes his features in the eyes of his partner" (p. 43); and, in effect, Leticia is finally able to say with conviction that Riquet is "the most handsome prince in the world." It is the same power of love which permits Anfino to see Penelope, in *The Dream Weaver*, as eternally young and beautiful. Riquet gradually becomes the "prince charming" of whose arrival through the gallery window Leticia has often dreamed while seated in the balcony of the palace playroom. It is here where, alone and unhappy, Leticia often played with a secret doll dressed as the handsome prince, whom Riquet has now become for her. "You are my beloved," she tells him, "whom I have sorrowfully awaited for years and who, at last, has come... to open my eyes" (p. 34).

Leticia's "blindness" however, occasionally returns; for at times she is unable to see the *handsome* Riquet, especially when others are present. Love's power to transform rests upon faith and Leticia's is imperfect. The alternative appearances of the two Riquets represent in visual form her constant conflict between faith and doubt and, also, Riquet's own. For his transformation depends, too, upon his own faith. "If you doubt yourself," Leticia asks him, "how shall I have faith? I attempt it, but I do not always succeed. Help me! For me, you will be the most elegant prince, as you are now... as long as you want to be" (p. 34). We have seen that it is Ulysses' lack of faith in his ability to please Penelope which prevents her from seeing in him the man she dreamed of. From doubt, however, the path leads to faith. When, after three months, Riquet must leave to visit his dying mother their mutual "test of faith" has been successful.

Riquet however, realizes that his absence will be a severe test and as he leaves Leticia as he found her, with the doll in her arms, he attaches to it a lock of his own red hair: "I want to prepare my conjuration, even though I doubt its efficacy. I will attempt to try to chain you to me. [...] Change back into a little girl, Leticia....Play with it [the doll] in my absence" (pp. 45-46). However, as Riquet has suggested, there are no charms and life is not a fairy tale. Only moments after his departure, Leticia awakens from her dreams to meet the handsome prince Armando who comes to ask her hand in marriage; and as her eyes meet his the doll slowly falls from her arms.

In his remarks about the tragedy, Buero explains that, for Perrault, the princess's decision to marry Riquet was doubtless accompanied by disillusionment for, in his tale, he states that *"having reflected* on the perseverance of her beloved, on his discretion and all the good qualities of his soul and spirit, she no longer saw that his body was deformed and his face ugly."[26] [Italics Buero's.] "Perrault's tales," Buero continues, "often contain either disguised or openly tragic elements... together with rose color, something of blackness or skepticism." From the implicit "almost" of Perrault, "a realistic and judicious doubt, which far from diminishing the fairy-like quality of the anecdote, humanizes it," comes the explicit "almost" of Buero's tragedy, in which he attempts to "unite a bit of poetry and a bit of reality."

Once Leticia has glimpsed in Armando the fruits of the world and "their desirable but immediate and deceitful beauty," she is no longer able to see in Riquet the prince that was her ideal and his. The figure of Armando will always be between them. When Riquet returns after three months, only by closing her eyes can she see him as handsome. In a scene in which the ugly and the handsome Riquets appear to her simultaneously, the ugly Riquet questions whether her love was only an illusion or lie, while the handsome Riquet affirms its truth:

THE UGLY RIQUET: Couldn't it all have been an illusion without stability? Or perhaps a lie! A clever lie forged before she suspected that another man could court her!

THE HANDSOME RIQUET: No. Her expression didn't deceive me. She found me pleasing and she loved me . . .

THE UGLY RIQUET: And now she no longer loves me. Oh God, God! What are we like? What are we really like? Each one sees us differently. How do You see us? How do You see me? What am I for You?

THE HANDSOME RIQUET: Handsome?

THE UGLY RIQUET: Horrible? . . . (*He runs his hands nervously over his face.*) You see me as You have made me. Horrible. That is the way others always saw me, and now she is right.
THE HANDSOME RIQUET: Or perhaps not? Your truth, Lord, is an infinite love for all things. She loved me and, because she did, I was her ideal. Who can triumph over an ideal?
THE UGLY RIQUET: Armando . . . (*A brief pause.*)
THE HANDSOME RIQUET: I won't resign myself! We'll have a showdown. I'll fight for her . . . (pp. 59-60)

The basic theme of Buero's play goes beyond that of the old myth of "beauty and the beast," in its most elementary sense. The underlying question here, as in romantic writer Edmond Rostand's *Cyrano de Bergerac*, Buero states, is not so much a sentimental question of beauty and ugliness, as of "the essence of the human personality: the doubt as to what we can essentially become in view of what we circumstantially seem to be."[27] Buero explains that he chose the present tale of "Riquet" because "in it the theme of personality implies a multiple development— for Riquet's self-questioning, when he asks how and what he really is, is related to an identical self-questioning on the part of the princess about herself"—but also because of the technical challenge provided by the possibility of the repeated alternation of two actors representing a single person.[28]

When Leticia finally "decides" to accept Riquet as her husband, it is not as the prince of her dreams, but the "buffoon." In a review, Haro Tecglen states that "illusion is replaced by disillusion and the effect of a charm by the weight of reason"— ideas, which as we have seen, Buero considers implicit in Perrault's tale.[29] As Riquet warns Leticia, her decision will bring suffering: "The pain will begin now. The pain of our sad intimacy. . . . Our union will be eternal agony amidst pavanes, endless weeping amidst the laughter of damsels" (p. 72).

Despite the sorrow it entails, Leticia prefers the real love of Riquet, who has made her "live again," to the superficial attentions of the handsome but vacuous Armando who, like others in the court, considers her stupid and inferior to himself—as, indeed, he considers all women. Armando, moreover, who is as blind as was Ulysses to the real meaning of love, wants to marry Leticia primarily for political advantage. Here, as in the preceding two plays, egoistic love is contrasted to pure disinterested love.

Armando tells Leticia: "Princes marry for many reasons. . . . For them affection is something different . . . and more judicious than for common people." The superficiality of Armando's love is, indeed, indicative of his attitude toward life in general. Like Ulysses he is the egoistic "reasoner" for whom the object of life is to further his own interest. Life, in short, is like the game of cards to which, confident of his own superiority, he invites Riquet in order to degrade him in Leticia's eyes. "In the gallant century in which we live, why think of antiquated manifestations of hostility? Elegance is preferable. . . . Isn't our century admirable, gentlemen? The century which has attained to the difficult virtue of turning life into a game" (p. 63). For Riquet, however, life is real. The game therefore becomes a duel.

Riquet then kills Armando in the duel provoked by the latter—a duel in which his nobility is so resplendent that for once, the only time in the play, all present see him, to their astonishment, as the imposing prince Leticia once saw. When Riquet prepares to leave, realizing that the charm has not worked and that Leticia, despite her protests to the contrary, no longer sees him as she did before, she explains to him the reason for her decision: "I prefer that sorrow [. . .] to the horror of some other Armando. To the vain and fleeting illusion of another brutal and icy man like him, who might make me foolish and frivolous like he wanted me to be" (p. 72).

By choosing the real love of Riquet, the fulfillment of which she knows will be difficult if not impossible, Leticia wins an internal victory quite similar to Penélope's. She accepts the difficult truth of Riquet's ineffaceable ugliness as she decides to "look for the charm again . . . although in pain and grief," and to continue to appear stupid to the court, although she isn't. It is her inner ennoblement which enables Leticia, like Penelope, to live in hope, although she can no longer see the handsome prince that is her ideal:

LETICIA: Let us love each other in that ideal! Let us in it dream
    together of our sad truth.
RIQUET: May the memory of it guide us and help us. . . . It will for-
    ever await us, unattainable, in the depths of our hearts.
LETICIA: Yes. It awaits us, from some world without sorrow. My
    gentle, sweet, ugly Riquet. . . . Come. (p. 72)

One critic states that "Buero affirms, under the stylized surface of the fairy tale, the necessity for the acceptance of suffering as a foundation of hope."[30]

The transformation of the handsome Riquet that Leticia can no longer see into an ideal which she remembers and into a symbol of hope for the future is shown by a skillful visual effect. During the preceding dialogue between the ugly Riquet and the princess, the handsome Riquet appears in the gallery window with an expression "charged with pain, nostalgia and distance." It is in front of this "unattainable figure, which in its ideal depth of music and dreams, will always preside over their difficult love," that Leticia kisses the lips of the ugly Riquet as the curtain falls. It is of this "unattainable figure" that Leticia will continue to dream; for dreams are necessary in Buero Vallejo's poetic world, a major characteristic of which, states critic Jean-Paul Borel, is "a passion for the impossible."[31] This play, like *The Dream Weaver*, ends tragically, that is, with a desperate hope.

Almost a Fairy Tale, like *The Words in the Sand* and *The Dream Weaver*, contrasts blind egoism and incomprehension with pure disinterested love and human understanding. In all three plays, we have seen that this contrast is developed by the use of sets of opposing characters, a technique which Buero uses in many of his works. The egoist, usually the practical man of action, is contrasted with the idealist or dreamer. Asaf is opposed to Jesus; Ulysses, to Anfino; and Armando, to Riquet. In *The Dream Weaver* and *Almost a Fairy Tale*, moreover, there is an additional contrast between Ulysses and Penelope and Armando and Leticia in that the women, also, are visionaries or dreamers. Penelope's vision of a day in which there will be "a universal promise," or a "bond of love" corresponds to Leticia's dream of the "world without sorrow" where the handsome Riquet, transformed into an ideal which she will remember, awaits her. Penelope, indeed, represents a sort of dreamer-protagonist very frequent in Buero's theater.

The Dream Weaver is significant, also, in that, interwoven with the major theme of love and understanding, are suggestions of additional ideas quite important to Buero's theater. Strong antiwar sentiment, particularly, is seen in Penelope's condemnation of the contest fought "because men . . . reasoned and decided that, in order to avenge the honor of a poor idiot named Menelao, it was necessary to spill blood in a war that lasted ten years."[32] Important also, is the metaphysical emphasis seen at the conclusion of the play, after Anfino's death, when Penelope professes her faith that she will accompany him, one day, in another world where he awaits her and dreams of her eternal beauty. Penelope, like many of Buero's characters, even in those plays nearer the social than the metaphysical pole of his theater, conveys a consciousness of the mystery which lies beyond man's grasp and the possibility of a transcendent reality to which many men are spiritually blind.

All three tragedies are illustrative of the diversity of technique in the playwright's theater. In the search for eternal truth about man which tragedy proposes, many techniques are valid. Through the re-creation of biblical episode and Greek myth, that is, through a return to an historical or legendary past, Buero treats themes relevant to all ages. At times reality, with its imponderable mystery, may best be revealed through fairy tale or fantasy. Buero has commented that fantasy "may disclose a tremendous reality."[33] It may show that reality has more than one plane, as in *Almost a Fairy Tale*, which confronts us with the double reality of the ugly and the handsome princes. Fantasy, Buero continues, does not "try to deny the crudeness of the ordinary plane of reality on which we dwell, but to [. . .] reveal it." Indeed, most of Buero's plays may be termed many-faceted for the multiplicity of the planes of reality they present and the questions they raise. "Perhaps all art," Buero suggests, "is nothing more than an inquiry into the mystery of reality."[34]

CHAPTER 4

The Search for Meaningful Human Relationships

"Pilar, Pilar! . . . You meant everything to me
and now I'm alone."
—*Hoy es fiesta* (*Today's a Holiday*)[1]

I N addition to the three tragedies discussed in the preceding
chapter, five other plays of Buero deal primarily with the
problem of meaningful personal relationships—*Madrugada*
(*Dawn*), 1953; *La señal que se espera* (*The Awaited Sign*), 1952;
Hoy es fiesta (*Today's a Holiday*), 1956; *Las cartas boca abajo*
(*The Cards Face Down*), 1957; and *La doble historia del doctor Valmy* (*The Double Case History of Doctor Valmy*), 1968.
These plays deal particularly with man's search for the truth
about his relationships with others or with his attempt to evade
this truth. This problem of seeking or avoiding truth in human
relationships has been seen to some extent, in the preceding
plays. Asaf and Ulysses, particularly, are defeated precisely because of their unwillingness to face the darkness of their egoism,
their lack of generosity and compassion. Both prefer to perpetuate comfortable fictions rather than confront the reality of their
situation. This problem of man's willingness or unwillingness
to search for truth becomes a predominant theme in the five
plays to be treated. In *Dawn* and *The Awaited Sign* especially,
we see, in a very explicit manner, the tragic protagonists' search
for the illumination upon which a deeper understanding may be
based. Even though there exists the risk that the truth which
the protagonists seek may result as painful and difficult to face,
it is only after its acceptance that the ground is cleared for the
possibility of any genuine hope.

I Madrugada (Dawn)

Dawn depicts the tragic struggle of the protagonist, Amalia,
to learn what Buero has termed the "inner truth" of her mar-

riage.[2] The entire work deals with her desperate but seemingly
hopeless attempt to clarify her husband's feelings toward her.
Amalia's husband Mauricio, a wealthy artist, has just died as the
play begins. Immediately before, he has married Amalia, who
was his model and mistress, and left her virtually his entire
fortune. Amalia is tormented by doubts as to whether this was
to prove his love or merely to pay her for her past services. Her
doubts arise from her suspicions that Mauricio may have believed slanderous statements probably made by one of his relatives. If this were the case, she would be able to explain certain
enigmatic words her husband uttered before his death and the
omission from his will of a bequest to the man who had tried to
seduce her: "Nothing for Leandro, for that scoundrel who stole
his [Maurico's] wife, or for his father, just in case. For the
sinful woman, yes. For her, benevolence, pardon, scorn. Payment
perhaps" (p. 14). She must learn if this omission signifies jealousy
of her and scorn, or to the contrary, trust and love.

   Amalia had tried unsuccessfully to reach an understanding
with Mauricio before his death. She tells her maid and confi-
dant, Sabina: "When we were alone, I tried to clear things up!
. . . It was difficult. [. . .] My timidity stood in the way. The shame
I felt in bringing up such a delicate matter. . . . This cursed shame
of mine which has prevented us from creating the necessary trust
in each other" (p. 15). The strange words which her husband
uttered on that occasion have increased Amalia's doubts:

AMALIA: Then he said something . . . tremendous. "It is too late to
        say many things, my poor Amalia. . . . But perhaps, I will
        win you back from beyond the grave." [. . .] I began to weep,
        telling him: "But you have not lost me." And he answered
        me: "No, I haven't lost you. But, perhaps I'll win you back
        . . . from the other side." . . . (A pause.) I threw myself into
        his arms and asked him what he meant. . . . He died. (Wrought
        up.) What did he mean?
SABINA: Perhaps he suspected your doubts and wanted to reassure
        you . . .
AMALIA: No. It was something concrete. Something in his words that
        sounded like an infinite sweetness. . . .Pardon, perhaps? Pardon
        for something I haven't done? (Bitter.) If that is the case,
        I'll be completely lost. (p. 15)

Sabina suggests that Mauricio somehow, even now, is able to hear Amalia's words of explanation and love. For Amalia, however, Mauricio's love means everything and she must somehow clarify his words: "It seems as if he himself orders me to do it! [. . .] I cannot live a moment longer, without trying to let him win me back . . . forever" (p. 16).

Almost the entire tragedy portrays the intricate and well-planned battle of wits in which Amalia engages her husband's relatives, whom she summons in a desperate scheme to learn the truth. She tells the relatives, who do not know that Mauricio has just died, that he is ill and expected to die shortly, but that she will not have him sign the will leaving her his fortune if they will give her certain information, if they will tell her who vilified her, and how Mauricio reacted. A woman of amazing willpower, Amalia finds in her love for the man who has elevated and redeemed her the strength to struggle for the knowledge without which she cannot live. She insists upon learning the truth despite the anguish which her efforts will entail and despite the risk that the truth may not be that for which she hopes. In Buero's theater, it has been commented, "the tragedy of man implicit in the knowledge and exercise of free will is always preferable to the ignorance and complacency of spiritual blindness."[3]

Dawn presents several interesting parallels with Ibsen's *Ghosts*. Both dramas deal with the tragic quest of the protagonist for her true inner self, for a clearer realization of the meaning of her past. Whereas *Dawn* depicts Amalia's struggle for enlightenment about her marriage, *Ghosts* portrays Mrs. Alving's anguished search for the nature and causes of the incurable illness of her son, who returns home from his studies just as the tragedy begins. Both protagonists gain new insights as a result of their probings. The underlying form of *Ghosts* is that of "the tragic rhythm as one finds it in *Oedipus Rex*,"[4] which portrays the hero's search for the murderer of his father. Ibsen, like the Greek tragedian, shows only the end of this quest, when the past is being brought up again in the light of the present. The same is true in the case of *Dawn*, which, as we have seen, begins immediately after the death of the protagonist's husband.

Dawn, like *Ghosts*, proceeds somewhat like detective stories, with mounting intrigue and suspense, as Amalia exhumes the past. Elements which underscore the mounting tension during her contest with the relatives are, first, the presence, offstage, of the dead body, with the imminent risk of its discovery by the relatives, and, second, the pressure of time. Since Amalia knows that, in an hour and a half, the friends who will come to arrange the wake will reveal that Mauricio is already dead, she essays to trick the guilty person into betraying himself under the stress of the minutes which tick by. The relatives, meanwhile, try to prolong the battle in the hope that Mauricio will die before signing the will, and two of them even plot to murder him. A clock on stage continues ticking away, visibly marking the identification of theatrical time with real time.

When the tragedy begins, the clock shows the time as a quarter past four in the morning; and when the final curtain falls, it strikes six. The clock runs throughout the entire drama, including a fifteen-minute intermission, during which the characters retire to the dining room for coffee. The entire action of the play takes place in the adjoining living room not far from Mauricio's deathbed. The classic unities are thus observed to their limitation as the action of the play indeed requires. José María de Quinto has commented that "the realization of *Dawn* as far as its formal elements are concerned, authorizes us to point to Buero Vallejo as the most skillful craftsman of the contemporary Spanish stage."[5] De Quinto notes, also, that Buero avoids what could have been a facile trick in that he reveals to the spectator, from the very beginning, the real situation of the drama: that Amalia already has the money left her in the will and that her husband is already dead.

There is, in the play, perfect fusion between subject matter and form, the same integrated structure of Sophoclean tragedy. One critic states that, except for the absence of fatality, oracles, and vengeful gods from Buero Vallejo's play, the technique employed in *Dawn* is exactly that of *Oedipus Rex*.[6] Buero Vallejo comments, in turn: "The role of fate in the work is made indirect through the irreversibility of the painter's death, that of the Oracle through the premonitory words he utters to Amalia, and that of the vengeful gods through the indifferent clock, an ancient bearded Cronus which by its very presence ensnares various characters in their own errors and precipitates them toward a crime."[7]

In the course of Amalia's tragic search, the jealousy, greed, and hatred of the relatives gradually come to light. Leandro envies Mauricio for his artistic achievements and for his success in winning Amalia's love. Lorenzo, his brother Dámaso, and the latter's wife Leonor all covet the money Amalia will inherit. Leonor, moreover, scorns Amalia for her former role as Mauricio's mistress. Magaña de Schevill remarks that the play "contrasts the egoism, hypocrisy, and false morality of the husband's family with the noble sentiments of the woman who has sinned and whom they humiliate and despise."[8] The ethical emphasis of our Western tradition, which is a major characteristic of all of Buero's theater, is obvious—just as it is in three tragedies of the preceding group.

Only minutes before the final curtain does Amalia learn the truth which she so tragically seeks. And this truth signifies the complete triumph of her love. Mauricio omitted Leandro and Lorenzo from his will because they had both slandered her. Lorenzo had told him that she was seeing Leandro; and Leandro had written an anonymous letter stating that she was seeing a former lover—a letter which Mauricio returned upon learning that Leandro had lied. Amalia now understands that Mauricio's "silence," his omission of their names from his will, thus signifies trust and confidence: "A silence which does not mean jealousy as I feared at first; a silence which does not implicate the father and son because the latter had seduced his wife, but because both insulted her. A silence which revives me, which returns him to me, which wins him back from beyond death" (p. 79). In *Dawn,* unlike the first three plays discussed, love wins out over greed, envy, resentment, and hatred.

Amalia's triumph, moreover, has a positive effect upon the relatives, who have tried to disgrace and humiliate her. As the result of the self-understanding which they achieve, they display a dignity which they previously lacked. Dámaso speaks for all as he admonished his wife: "May this be a lesson to both of us." Alfonso Sastre, in a review of the play published in *Cuadernos Hispanoamericanos,* speaks of the cathartic impact of the drama, which he calls a "harsh and purifying work."[9]

In *Dawn,* as in *Ghosts,* the clear vision or insight attained by the protagonists is symbolized at the end by the bright morning light. Whereas most of Ibsen's play takes place while the land-

scape is shrouded in mist and rain, the tragedy ends with a view
of the sunlight on the mountain peaks and glaciers. However,
the truth which Mrs. Alving has attained is a damning vision.
She realizes that she herself caused her husband's profligacy and
destroyed his joy and vitality with her strict code of morality.
She herself is thus partially responsible for the syphilis which
her son Oswald has inherited from his father.[10] Her hopes both
to save her son from the "ghosts" of the past and to find a new
life of joy and freedom for herself are destroyed.

Dawn concludes with a stage effect which is quite similar.
After the relatives leave, Amalia turns off the lamp, letting in
the morning sunlight, which floods the room, dissipating the
shadows: "Her expression is now beautiful: it reveals a super-
human calm and a boundless love. . . . She approaches the large
window and draws back the curtains. The pure clear light of
dawn penetrates the living room" (p. 81). The truth reached by
Amalia, unlike that attained by Mrs. Alving, signifies the fulfillment of all her hopes. Love has triumphed and the dawn
announces the termination of her doubts and fears. The tragedy
thus stands at that pole of the tragic spectrum which Buero
Vallejo describes as "that of faith without a shadow of doubt
. . . that of hope fulfilled."[11]

II   La señal que se espera (The Awaited Sign)

Enrique in *The Awaited Sign*,[12] unlike Ulysses in *The Dream
Weaver*, is a man of doubt and jealousy, of spiritual blindness.
He unjustly suspects that his wife, Susana, has married him
only for his money and that she still cares for her former sweet-
heart, Luis. Susana believes that it is Enrique whom she loves,
but she is not absolutely certain of this; and Luis still enter-
tains some hope that Susana loves him. The tragedy consists of
the efforts of these three major characters to learn the truth
about their relationships with one another.

In a desperate effort to learn the truth, Enrique, who hopes
for an assurance of his wife's love, forces an encounter between
Susana and Luis, bringing the latter to his Galician summer
house to recuperate from a nervous breakdown caused by the
failure of his marriage. He also permits Luis, a musician who
has been unable to compose since he was abandoned by Susana,

to construct an aeolian harp. As Buero explains during the course of the tragedy, this is a harp which emits, with changes in the atmosphere, sounds similar to a crude type of music. Luis says that he hopes the harp will miraculously play a forgotten melody as a sign that his work may begin again. This melody, we learn later, is a song which he wrote for Susana shortly before she left him for Enrique. Vaguely remembering a piece which he heard Susana play during the early days of their courtship, and perhaps suspecting that this is what Luis expects to hear, Enrique permits him to construct the harp; for he fears that if Susana does love Luis, she may play it herself to make this miracle happen.

Enrique's struggle is paralleled by that of Susana, both to prove her love for her husband and to verify his love in her own mind. This struggle is complicated by the responsibility which she feels toward Luis. Luis, Enrique, and Susana, who seem unable to communicate their true feelings, all long for understanding in their relationship with each other. Without realizing it until later, Julián, a guest, hopes for the return of his wife who has left him for another man. All the characters, with varying degrees of faith, are hoping for something. The old Galician servants, Rosenda and Bernardo, who are childless, dream of news from a nephew who left years ago. Reasssured by tío Carmelo, an old shepherd wise in witchcraft and magic, they believe that Luis' melody will be the sign that they will receive a letter.

"We all hope," Julián remarks, even though there may be no rational probability of realizing this hope. It is hope which brings Luis and the servants to the garden at sunset, the hour when the atmospheric conditions are most propitious, to listen for the music of the harp, which is set up in the adjoining sun porch. Each of the three acts takes place at this same time on a different summer afternoon. The entire tragedy thus centers on this moment when all the characters listen, either consciously or subconsciously, for the melody: the group in the garden consisting of the servants, Luis, and Susana, who accompanies the latter out of sympathy, and, inside, Julián and Enrique.

As a result of the responsibility which Susana feels toward Luis, she finally decides to play the melody which she believes to be the one for which he is waiting. Her motives are not en-

tirely clear even to her. Somehow, though, she feels that the
time has come to end the tension of everyone, including Enrique.
Enrique's reaction is indicative of his struggle between faith
and doubt. When he learns, first, that Susana has been seen
running toward the beach to drown herself, he believes this to
be a sign that she loves him; for she had once said that her
disappearance would be the ultimate proof of her affection. But
when, minutes later, he hears the music of the harp,[13] which she
has secretly come back to play, his doubts return. In the end,
however, his tenacious efforts to learn the truth are rewarded.
Susana gives proof of her love by choosing to remain with him
despite the news of his complete financial failure, about which
he had learned in a letter received early in the play, but which
he does not reveal until near the end.

Whereas the path of Enrique toward Susana is one of doubt,
the path of Susana toward Enrique is one of faith. As she explains later, she plays the melody with the belief Enrique will
somehow understand: "I have faith, and it was because of my
faith that I did not reach the beach. I knew that you were
going to misinterpret it, and I trusted that, in spite of everything, you would understand ... some day" (p. 52). And by
playing the harp, Susana clears up her own lingering doubts
as to whom she loves; for as she plays Luis' melody, she thinks
of Enrique.

Enrique and Susana succeed in reaching an understanding
because they seek it by positive actions and by faith. Enrique's
doubts are only the negative side of the faith which Susana reads
in his eyes: "I hope. I hope! ... because your eyes show your
faith in me [...] in spite of everything" (p. 53). Buero has
pointed out that it is possible for the tragic protagonist to win a
victory over destiny when, distrusting the inexorability of fate and
placing his hope in his own ability, he seeks it with acts of free
will and by faith.[14] Enrique's attempt to test his wife's fidelity
by bringing into their home her former fiancé is, in a sense, as
imprudent and nearly disastrous as Ulysses' spying upon Penelope. Enrique, however, succeeds because his efforts, unlike
Ulysses', are based upon faith. "Because he seeks enlightenment
so tenaciously," Buero remarks, "he will finally attain it."[15]

Luis' success in regaining his ability to work is also due to
faith. That he constructs the harp with the subconscious faith

that Susanna will play it, is evident in one of their conversations: "If you wait for it with me, it will come. [...] When I look in your eyes, I feel confident.... Will it sound this afternoon, Susana? [...] (*Almost threateningly.*) ... There's not much time left. Do you hear? There's not much time left!" (p. 29).

The theme of the tragedy is, thus, the creative power of faith, a theme also present in *The Dream Weaver* and especially, *Almost a Fairy Tale*. It is the hope and faith of all which bring the "sign" and the letters for the servants and for Julián, which arrive shortly afterwards, the "shared faith" of which Luis speaks just before the melody sounds: "The garden is abandoned. Now the invisible fingers of God can grant me my melody.... It's absurd, isn't it? But I believe! If the garden is empty, it is also encircled by a great faith! The servants ... prick up their ears and pray. Susana weeps in her room and listens.... And I wait for my sign" (p. 42). But it is more than the desire of the characters which brings the "sign" and the letters which Susana associates with it.

SUSANA: Then my hands played.... But, it's a mystery to me who produced the sign..., although these hands played.
ENRIQUE: (*Surprised.*) What are you saying?
SUSANA: Perhaps your own desire brought it, everyone's desire (*lowering her voice*) or perhaps an invisible and higher desire. (pp. 57-58)

Although played by human hands, the "sign" of the harp is, like Susana's return from the beach, a miracle. "Everything is a miracle," Julián observes. "The simple existence of things is one. A miracle is a plant that grows, even though it may not produce exotic flowers, and a harp and a cave where voices echo even though we think we know why they resound.... A miracle is a son who is conceived, is born, and becomes a man" (p. 23). "The mystery of things," Buero explains, "resides in these things without violating their outward appearances and does not imply exceptional miracles." The miracle of the harp, he states, cannot be manifested in a crudely ostensible manner, but the result of the melody is the same.[16]

Through the "sign," the characters gain an understanding of their past errors. Susana now realizes that her marriage almost failed because she and Enrique lacked something they should

have wanted but did not, a definite sign: "that miracle of a child."
Luis now understands that he forgot the melody in a subconscious effort to escape the truth, to forget his humiliation upon
being abandoned by Susana. To him the "sign" brings not happiness, but acceptance and strength to face a difficult future. To
Julián the "sign" brings the realization that the near failure of
his marriage was partially his own fault and the decision to
pardon his wife, who left him for another man, but who has now
written that she wants to return. "Perhaps," he realizes, "we all
have to forgive each other" (p. 54). He thus achieves the enlightenment which Asaf and Ulysses fail to. To Bernardo and
Rosenda, who learn from the letter that their nephew has died
remembering them, the "sign" brings peace.

Through the catharsis which the characters have undergone,
their tension has been resolved into spiritual peace and harmony.
This inner peace is manifest in a highly effective auditory device
near the end of the tragedy. As the six characters gather, Julián
remarks that the air is calm and that all is quiet. It must have
been moments like this, he says, which made the ancients believe
in the possibility of hearing the music of the spheres. And then
"The chords of a very sweet and distant harmony, which one
would say was made by eternally murmuring wind and clear
voices, begins to sound. It is a music which has not been created
and which does not exist on earth; but perhaps it may remotely
resemble Wagner's prelude to 'Lohengrin'" (p. 61). This music
continues until the curtain falls, enveloping the characters in its
harmony, as they experience what they feel to be a unique
moment which will perhaps never be repeated in their lives.[17]

This sound effect reinforces the metaphysical aspects of the
tragedy, reminding us of the inner and spiritual significance of
reality, of the mystery which constantly surrounds us. The
suggestion of the existence of a transcendent reality to which
man is usually spiritually blind is present in most of Buero's
plays. Indeed, the critic José Luis Abellán has stated: "A preoccupation with mystery and marvel is perhaps the constant
most characteristic of Buero's theater."[18] The tragedy thus ends
in triumph, confirming the declaration made earlier by Julián:
"Faith is never useless. . . . Faith moves mountains and produces
signs. It is through its power that we live" (p. 48). *The Awaited*

Sign, like *Dawn,* stands very near the affirmative pole of Buero's theater, near the pole of hope fulfilled.

III   Hoy es fiesta (Today's a Holiday)

Today's a Holiday deals with the efforts of Silverio, the protagonist, to reach an understanding with his wife, Pilar, to bridge the gap which separates him from her—efforts which come only after a long period of insincerity and evasion. For years Silverio has fled from his responsibility in the death of the daughter whom Pilar had by an enemy soldier before her marriage. His deliberate negligence was responsible, he believes, for the death of the little girl—whom he hated. Silverio longs to confess his guilt to Pilar; but he cannot believe that she could forgive him if she knew the truth. Like Luis, Susana, and Enrique in *The Awaited Sign,* Silverio is unable to communicate his problems. His guilt, which he has never had the courage to confess to her, is the barrier which stands between them.

One day, however, Daniela, one of Silverio's neighbors in the Madrid tenement house where he lives, forces him to face his problem. When she is berated by her disagreeable mother for consulting a fortune teller about a problem in her life of poverty and anguish, Silverio sees in her eyes the childlike innocent expression of Pilar's daughter and understands that, without realizing it, he has always longed and hoped for pardon. He now confesses his past insincerity in his wife's presence. Pilar, however, cannot hear him for she is deaf.

SILVERIO: I've tried to deceive myself . . . devoting my life to you instead of telling you the truth I owed you, abandoning my ambitions and seeking refuge among these humble people to try to become just another one of them, as if I were fleeing some implacable eye which was always fixed on me. But it was useless, because that look . . . was yours.
[. . . . .]
I need your forgiveness, because I love you! . . . I'm lost! Because I know that you could never, never give it to me . . . if you knew it.

PILAR: Don't shout. Calm yourself! (*Nervously she looks in her pocket and takes out a notebook and pencil and offers them to him.*) Don't suffer alone! Tell me! What is that thing you're keeping to yourself?

SILVERIO: (*He looks at the notebook with boundless longing and terror.*) If only I dared . . .
PILAR: Tell me . . .
SILVERIO: I can't![19]

Thus we see in Silverio the same evasion which we saw in Luis, who sought to escape the reality of his abandonment by Susana. Although Silverio possesses the lucidity to see clearly both his past errors and his present cowardliness, he lacks the courage to communicate his problems to his wife. The lack of communication between the couple is symbolized dramatically by Pilar's deafness and by the constant presence of the notebook which she offers Silverio but which he lacks the courage to write on.

Today's a Holiday is more than the individual tragedy of Silverio. It is the collective tragedy of his neighbors in the tenement house, many of whom are popular types from the old Spanish *sainete* or short farce—for example, Nati, the portress, Sabas, the *chulo* or dude, and the good-hearted neighbor woman, Tomasa. Silverio is as isolated spiritually from all his neighbors as he is from his wife. Just as Silverio hopes for Pilar's forgiveness, all his neighbors in the tenement house hope for something to make their lives more bearable. Their hopes, however, assume the disguise of various illusions which life offers them in their poverty:[20] the realization of the prophecies of doña Nieves, the fortune teller, or the winning of the lottery prize, the announcement of which they are awaiting eagerly on this holiday. They dream of small, material things: a more cheerful apartment, a washing machine to make their burdens lighter, money for the movies, etc. The hopes these poor people invest in the lottery prize or the predictions of the fortune teller are as chimeric and irrational as the faith of Bernardo and Rosenda in the magical powers of tío Carmelo. In *Today's a Holiday*, however, unlike in *The Awaited Sign*, the author shows all the absurdity and the radical insufficiency of this type of hope which depends entirely upon chance for its fulfillment. Nevertheless, as Jean-Paul Borel points out in his *El teatro de lo imposible*, Buero never damns this hope,[21] for it is what permits these people to live. Without a minimum of hope, life would be impossible. As one neighbor expresses it, "man lives by hope." As another exclaims, "What the hell, one has to hope. If not, what would become of us?"

It is these hopes which bring together all the characters on the terrace rooftop to await the draw of the lottery when they find that the door, normally kept locked by the portress, has been inadvertently left open. The entire tragedy takes place on a holiday, between sunrise and sunset, when the characters sit in small groups to take the sun, to discuss their dreams, and to encourage one another. Just as *The Awaited Sign* focuses on the wait for the miracle of the sign, *Today's a Holiday* centers on the long wait for the newspaper which will announce, the characters believe, the miracle of the lottery prize. In *Today's a Holiday*, as in *The Awaited Sign*, hope forms an explicit theme; and as in the last tragedy, it appears on both the earthly and the transcendent plane—planes which, we shall see, merge one with the other.

The herald of hope in *Today's a Holiday* is doña Nieves who reads the future in her cards: "one must hope . . . one must always hope. . . . Hope never ends. . . . Let us believe in hope. . . . Hope is infinite" (p. 21). The role of doña Nieves is thus similar to the role of Julián in *The Awaited Sign;* and her declaration of hope, heard on various occasions when she consults the cards for her clients, may be compared to his. ("Faith is never useless. . . . Faith moves mountains. . . .") The fact that this declaration takes the form of an incantation uttered by a foolish, simpleminded fortune teller points up the often ambiguous and ironical nature of hope, an aspect of hope not known in *The Awaited Sign.*

On this holiday a miracle does happen, but not the miracle of the lottery prize. The numbers of the shares which the neighbors have bought from doña Balbina, Daniela's mother, turn out to be the winning ones. Balbina, however, as Daniela soon discloses, has deceived them with an old ticket in order to keep from starving. The real miracle, one more transcendent than a lottery prize, is the neighbors' forgiveness. As the result of the intervention of Silverio, the tenement dwellers, who in their first violent reaction have beaten Balbina, all turn over to him their lottery receipts and agree not to denounce her to the authorities. As Silverio says, "They've got hearts of gold, after all."

After the neighbors' initial disillusionment and bitterness, hope returns. They have lost the money of which they dreamed, but not their hopes, as is evident in the words of Tomasa: "Come on, Manola! (*She touches her on the shoulder.*) At the next drawing I'll buy you a ticket! And tomorrow I'll pay to have the cards read, for they're going to tell us very good things! ... One day everything will turn out right. You'll see!" (p. 89). Moreover, as the result of their kindness to Balbina, the neighbors have more reason to hope than before. For, as one critic has stated: "The door is at least partially ajar, to trust in the future and to the consolation of mutual solidarity."[22] As Pilar expresses it, "Today heaven has showered all its smiles upon this house" (p. 95).

After having persuaded doña Balbina's victims to forgive her, and after having saved her daughter Daniela from committing suicide, Silverio feels himself spiritually united with his neighbors for the first time. Moreover, the miracle which has taken place in the lives of all the neighbors on this day of euphoria and violence is a sign that he, too, may hope. For perhaps Pilar will somehow be able to forgive him, just as the neighbors have forgiven Balbina: "For me, today's a real holiday, a day to rejoice. What has happened is like a sign that I, too, ... can hope" (pp. 89-90).

For Silverio, this day is a special one, a day when, as the result of having helped his neighbors, he feels in harmony with the universe. It is a day when, even earlier, he has believed, despite his doubts, that hope and happiness are still possible: "Everything in life is so obscure and mysterious ... and men, so insignificant .... Perhaps each man has only one day, or a few days of intuition and of kindness" (p. 53). Pilar, also, has known somehow, with the intuitive understanding which seems to compensate for her deafness, that this would be a unique day, a day of special beauty, when the evils of the world would dissolve into love and peace:

It's a beautiful day ... (*She walks around.*) It's especially clear. The fact is that some days are strange ... (*He [Silverio] stops and looks at her.*) Days in which it seems as if time has stopped or as if something important were going to happen. Don't you feel this way sometimes? As if things aren't familiar any longer ... As if one were seeing them for the first time and they were all very beautiful . . . The neighbors are good people even though they themselves don't know it; the witch is nice precisely when she makes a sour face, because one knows that she's only a poor woman who doesn't understand anything and heaven is full of pity for her. And even this broken junk is pretty. . . . It's as if everything possessed a big smile that caressed it. (p. 38)

There is suggested here, as in *The Awaited Sign,* the presence of a world of mystery and marvel. This transcendent reality, symbolized in the first tragedy by the celestial music at the end, is perhaps shown in *Today's a Holiday* by the sunlight which falls on the terrace roof of the squalid tenement: "Everything is old, peeling, and tarnished [. . .] a broken three-legged stool. Next to the chimney, on the right, a box that's broken into pieces, a cracked flowerpot and an old dented washbowl. But upon all of it, the marvel of the morning sky and the tenderness of the sun which obliquely kisses from the right the rooftop tenements" (p. 9).

The metaphysical aspect beneath the surface of this play, classified by most critics as purely realistic, is evident, also, in the hopes of the neighbors. It is not really a lottery prize for which they hope in order to alleviate their anguish, but something more transcendental. That their hunger is spiritual as well as material is revealed in their eagerness to ascend to the terrace roof, normally forbidden them by the portress, in order to breathe "a purer, loftier air." And as a result of the miracle of their goodness to Balbina, this hunger is, to some degree, satisfied.

A spiritual door is opened for Silverio, also, on this holiday, this magical day when miracles seem possible. On this special day which is an anniversary of the death of Pilar's daughter, Silverio is enabled to compensate, in a sense, for his guilt by saving the life of Daniela. For Daniela, scorned by her mother who does not understand that she revealed the hoax of the lottery ticket only to save her from prison, and ignored by Fidel, a young neighbor whom she loves, is about to flee her problems by committing suicide when Silverio intervenes.

Silverio finally dares to hope that, by saving Daniela, he has somehow compensated for his responsibility in the death of Pilar's daughter; but he realizes that the final answer must come from his wife. As the result of this cathartic experience which he has undergone, he finally resolves, after years of silence, to confess his guilt. His hope, Borel points out, is not escapist or passive, like that of the other characters.[23] His hope, like that of Susana and Enrique in *The Awaited Sign,* is an active force which leads to positive action. However, Silverio's determination to reach an understanding with his wife comes too late. Before he can write his confession in his wife's notebook, an act which would break down the barrier between them and perhaps bind them together definitively, Pilar dies unexpectedly as a result of a blow received during the altercation over doña Balbina.

There is a moment preceding Pilar's death which reminds us of the moment of spiritual peace and serenity near the end of *The Awaited Sign.* "Don't you feel it?" asks Pilar. "It's like a great joy that envelops the two of us ... like an immense river engulfing me" (pp. 95-96). However, Silverio, unlike the characters in *The Awaited Sign,* does not attain this peace, for he cannot be sure of Pilar's pardon. He must continue to live in doubt. To his question there is no answer: "Perhaps you can hear me at last with your poor dead ears .... Perhaps you already know. And I, how will I know? Only your lips can tell me if I am forgiven. Only your lips .... Pilar, Pilar! ... You meant everything to me and now I'm alone" (p. 96). The tragedy concludes as we hear once again the words of doña Nieves, the herald of hope, of the supernatural, of another world: "One must hope ... always hope.... Hope never ends.... Hope is infinite" (p. 96).

Buero remarks, in his commentary, that these final words may represent a great truth, an important affirmation—the infinite hope that somehow, at some time, Pilar will be able to hear Silverio's confession and pardon him. But these words, which come as Pilar dies, may also be merely the senseless incantation of an ignorant fortune teller which ironically underscores Silverio's despair. The title, likewise, Buero comments, may be either affirmative or brutally ironic. In *Today's a Holiday* the dramatist thus emphasizes the ironic, ambiguous, and contradictory nature of hope and its frequent unattainability, whereas in *The Awaited Sign* he exalts the positive nature of hope. While the latter ends with hope fulfilled, the former ends with doubt,

with a question. "The work," Buero states, "develops and concludes in a vital ambivalence for which there is only one
unifying definition: an interrogatory one."[24] This ambivalence
is, of course, not synonymous with pessimism; because an attitude of hope on the part of an author is, for Buero Vallejo, the
sine qua non of tragedy.

IV   Las cartas boca abajo (The Cards Face Down)

In the words of one reviewer, *The Cards Face Down* is "the
mute but brutal contest of five beings confined between four
walls."[25] An entire family leads an existence of evasion and
insincerity, maintaining their cards face down. All failures, they
long for success and happiness, for escape from the asphyxiating
atmosphere of their old apartment with its peeling cornice and
its slowly widening cracks. In their spiritual blindness and
hypocrisy, however, they succeed only in destroying one another.
They are as unwilling to face the truth about themselves or to
attempt to clarify their relationships with one another as was
Silverio for many years. Juan, the husband, expresses this when
he states, "We are slowly sinking into silence."[26]

Adela, the protagonist, secretly detests her mediocre husband,
Juan, and dreams of Carlos Ferrer, an intellectual whom she
wanted to marry in her youth. She had succeeded in taking
him away from her sister, in whom he was interested, but he
had finally abandoned both of them. Adela had then married
Ferrer's friend, Juan, out of spite. For Adela, the passing years
with a husband whom she does not love have resulted in only
boredom and fear. In an attempt to escape this boredom to
which she cannot resign herself, Adela lives a fictitious life of
illusion, dreaming of her love for Ferrer. The free and joyous
life for which she longs is symbolized by the singing of the
birds from a nearby park which fly by the balcony every afternoon at sunset. In her desperate thirst for life, Adela has become
obsessed with their songs:

> They enchanted me when I was small. After I played in the
> afternoons, I would sit down to watch them ... It seemed to me
> that when I was older, I, too, would be free and joyful like them ...
> Such self-deception, isn't it? But they haven't changed. They return
> every afternoon, bringing joy to the house and making me feel like

a little girl again. I forget everything then and it seems to me that I still have hope ... They're not like us. They fly. They fight for their fledglings; sometimes they fall into the claws of their enemies. Yet they're always brimming with life as they accompany the sunset with a babble of song. They celebrate their delirious fiesta. They're the delight of the skies. The joy of a free life ... They are happy. (*The loud noise of their warbling fills the room ...*) (pp. 29-30)

Anita, the neurotic sister whose love for Ferrer has been thwarted by Adela, also secretly dreams of him and of the happiness which has escaped her. She has, moreover, carried her implacable resentment against Adela to the point of becoming permanently mute. The everpresent figure of Anita with her reproaching eyes represents a constant, tacit reminder of Adela's guilt. As her brother, Mauro, suggests to her: "Perhaps ... your conscience and Anita are one and the same thing." Anita has been compared to other accusing figures: the statue in the Don Juan plays, the silent friend, Miss Y, in Strindberg's *The Stronger,* and the old servant in Camus' *The Misunderstanding.*[27] Her silence gives occasion, moreover, to monologues, especially by Adela, who reveals her misery and need for pardon —which Anita is unable or unwilling to give. Adela's monologue is similar to Silverio's when he confesses his guilt to Pilar who cannot hear him. One critic states that with *The Cards Face Down* Buero restores the efficacy of the monologue proscribed from most realistic theater, but invaluable in revealing intimate feelings.[28] Equally important, however, Anita's silence, like Pilar's deafness, symbolizes the lack of communication between all the members of the family—and thus the radical solitude and incommunicability of man in general.

Juan, who has remained a lowly assistant professor, secretly envies his former companion, Ferrer, now a renowned scholar, as he makes a final, pathetic attempt to win a professorship at the age of fifty. Juanito, the son, despises his mediocre father and longs to leave home. Mauro, Adela's brother, a modern *pícaro* or rogue, who pilfers small objects in order to survive, no longer dreams. He is merely the mirror in which the others see their own failures. Although Carlos Ferrer never appears on stage, his figure acquires the dimensions of a myth, as Sáinz de Robles has noted. To Adela, he represents the love which she has never known; to Ana, the happiness which she has never felt; and to Juanito, the success for which he is striving.[29] The life together of Adela, Anita, Juan, and Juanito, each one immersed in his own solitude and unable to communicate his problems, is one of silent anguish and torture. This silence is, as one critic has stated, "the heart of the conflict": "the silence of guilt gravitating over their corrupted souls, strangling them with fear and loneliness."[30]

Part of the play deals with the unsuccessful efforts of Adela, who, like Silverio in *Today's a Holiday*, is obsessed with the idea of her guilt and desires to bridge the gap which separates her from her sister. The major part of the play, however, deals with the struggle of Juan, who, finally admitting the need for sincerity and clarity, tries to reach an understanding with his wife after the first day of examinations for the professorship:

JUAN: Both of us keep our cards face down instead of exposing them ... and, little by little, the game is ruined. It's possible they have already eliminated me. I don't know. But if we could try, from now on, to turn up some of those cards we keep hidden ... I wouldn't care too much.
ADELA: Don't always expect the worst.... We still don't know anything.
JUAN: You haven't given me a reply.
ADELA: To what?
JUAN: You see? You evade the question again. Our marriage is like a silent battle. (p. 33)

Juan's failure to win the professorship is the crisis or cathartic experience which causes him to make a final successful attempt to uncover his wife's cards. Letting her believe for a moment that he has actually won the professorship, he reads in her eyes what he has always feared: that she did not want him to win. He now understands that she married him not for love, but to spite Ferrer, who had rejected her: "You wanted to prove to ... someone else that, with your help, a man could get ahead.... And, when you couldn't prove it, you ended up hating me." It is due partially to Adela's scorn after Juan's first attempt to win the professorship that he has been unsuccessful in his subsequent attempts. To all this Adela has no answer: "What could I do! I never managed to distinguish my own impulses.... I did everything at the wrong time." Like Ibsen's

Hedda Gabler, who drives Loveborg to commit suicide, Adela
has dominated and destroyed all about her. In her boredom
and dissatisfaction with life, she has thwarted her sister's love,
attempted to use Juan as an instrument of revenge, and turned
Juanito against his father. As Fernández-Santos points out, "It is
she who becomes a catalyst to the drama with her hypocrisy,
her scorn, and her pride, revolving around a past she once
despised, and her egoism."[31]

The mediocre but noble Juan also exposes his own cards,
admitting his envy of Ferrer which prevented him from reading
several of the writer's works upon which he was questioned
during his examination: "Ferrer Díaz is a much better scholar
than I am. [...] My great mistake has been not daring to acknowledge this while ... I secretly envied him. But now I don't
mind admitting it. Today's experience has been sufficient. [...]
How simple it would have been to admire and read the books
of my old friend, Carlitos Ferrer, all these years" (p. 82). Juanito
also uncovers his cards, confessing his hatred of his father. Only
Anita remains silent, as if judging all of them.

Through the cathartic experience he has undergone, Juan
now realizes that he must permit Juanito to leave home to
study, as his son wants. Perhaps, in this way, he will be enabled
to avoid his father's mistakes and to succeed where his father
has failed. Juan, therefore, although he has failed in his attempt
to win the professorship, has won an internal victory. As the
result of the enlightenment or knowledge to which he has
attained, he makes the decision which enables him to recover
the love and respect of his son.

At the end of the play, Juan is spiritually united with his
son who now understands him for the first time. But between
Juan and Adela, as between Adela and Anita, there seems to
remain little hope for communication or unity. For Adela, whose
continuing blindness and egoism have been responsible for the
unhappiness of her entire family, there seems to remain only
fear of the future. The fear and terror she feels are symbolized
by the sound of the birds in the afternoon, which now acquires
a meaning different from the one it had previously:

MAURO: Some time ago I was leafing through a curious book. It stated
that birds sing joyfully in the morning because the sun is rising

and they await a day filled with delightful adventures . . .
They're like us . . . at the dawn of our lives: empty-headed.
But in the afternoon they don't sing.

ADELA: Can't you hear them?

MAURO: Those aren't songs. They're shrieks. They shriek with terror
. . . What you thought was a frenzy of joy is a frenzy of
fear . . . By the end of the day they've had time to remember
that they're subject to the law of life and death. As the sun
vanishes they doubt that it will return. Then they band together and circle madly, trying to stupefy themselves. But
it is too late. They want to sing and all they can do is shriek.
(pp. 85-86)

For Adela, as well as for Silverio in *Today's a Holiday,* the
future appears to hold only loneliness: "From now on, I'll be
by myself. . . . All by myself" (p. 87). The tragedy concludes as
the terrifying sound of the birds penetrates the room.

However, hope is not completely gone even for Adela because
Juanito, before leaving home, has said to her: "Listen to them
[the birds] sing. Whenever you hear them, you'll remember
me. Perhaps, one day, all of us in this house, will know that
happiness. I'll return to try to make it possible" (p. 87). In the
light of the interpretation which Mauro has just given to the
songs of the birds, this hope can be, of course, cruelly ironic.
The Cards Face Down, like *Today is a Holiday,* thus ends
ambivalently, that is, with a question, whose purpose is to move
the spectator deeply, to make him feel the problem of human
suffering—which is, for Buero Vallejo, a major purpose of tragedy.

V La doble historia del Doctor Valmy
(The Double Case History of Doctor Valmy)

In *The Double Case History of Doctor Valmy,* lack of communication takes a more radical form than in *Today is a Holiday*
or *The Cards Face Down.* It is represented by the recent impotence of the protagonist Daniel, a National Security policeman
in an imaginary country, Surelia, whose work involves the torture of political prisoners, but who has always kept the true
nature of what he does a secret from his wife. In a desperate
attempt to ascertain the truth about his problem, he consults
Dr. Valmy, the psychiatrist who is a narrator of the play. Daniel's
desire to learn the truth, however, does not prevent him from

yielding to insincerity and evasion, as he denies any relationship
between his condition and his work, even a recent incident in
which he was forced, against his wishes, to destroy a prisoner's
virility.

Daniel's illness, Dr. Valmy explains to him, is actually a self-
punishment or penitence: "What you have done is irreparable.
You can never restore that poor man's virility, and therefore
you have destroyed your own. Don't you see, it's something
of a paradox: your cure is precisely your illness."[32] His situation
is thus similar to that of Silverio in *Today's a Holiday,* who
abandons his ambition to paint and seeks anonymity among the
humble tenement dwellers in an unconscious effort to flee the
guilt he feels in the death of Pilar's daughter. Daniel's guilt,
however, is obviously infinitely greater than Silverio's. He must
either convince himself that his action was justified—which is
impossible, despite his protests as to its political necessity—or
admit that he has committed a monstrous deed. Even then,
Dr. Valmy states, his cure is doubtful; for what he has done
is irreparable. The only price high enough for the deed he has
committed is the one he is already paying, or a radical change
in himself and his life: abandonment of his job and the search
for a forgiveness he is unlikely to obtain.

Daniel's evasion, however, continues; for it is only after Mary
receives a visit from Lucila, a former student of hers whose
husband turns out to be the man Daniel has destroyed, does
Daniel confess, in answer to his wife's questions, the real nature
of his work. The change in Daniel described by Dr. Valmy
seems possible, however, when he admits to Mary the causes
of his impotence and seeks her help in becoming the "other
man" he feels inside. This assistance she gladly offers, feeling
that sincerity and truthfulness between them will make everything possible: "I'll help you! I'll help you get out of that trap.
We can do it if we don't hide anything else from each other!
(*She sobs in his arms.*) We will, Daniel.... We will" (p. 134).
Even then, however, Daniel refuses to abandon the justifications
for torture which he has fabricated in order to be able to do his
job, the same justifications he expressed to Dr. Valmy. The police,
he rationalizes, do what they do not out of cruelty, but out of
necessity. Without them, in terrible times of uprisings and insur-
rection, the nation would not survive.

It is not only Daniel, however, who is guilty of insincerity. A similar evasion is seen on the part of Mary when she refuses to believe that torture is used despite Lucila's testimony to the contrary and despite the book on the history of torture which she is sent by the latter. She is likewise anxious to believe, until Daniel admits the truth, that he is not like the other police, that his role has been limited to that of an accomplice: "An accomplice because you have no choice . . . just as I have been an accomplice out of ignorance" (p. 135). As Lucila points out in answer to Mary's protests that there are laws and courts and that, if torture were used, it would be known: "Many people are determined that no one will know about it. And many others are determined not to know it. (*Looks away.*) Like you" (p. 122).

This evasion and escapism is perhaps symbolized by the song from a television commercial sung various times by the near-deaf Grandmother. The Grandmother clearly suspects the truth about her son's occupation, but prefers to avoid it since she herself was responsible for his joining the police: "Take Finus pills for all your pains/ And you'll be laughing soon again . . ." (p. 98). To Mary's pleas that the Grandmother help her son escape the trap into which he has fallen, she answers that she cannot hear anything being said, a reply belied by her pained expression and damp eyes. The Grandmother's deafness symbolizes our evasion of reality. "Perhaps at this moment another wretch is in there screaming," suggests Dr. Valmy. "But of course, we don't hear him. Our lack of concern makes us as deaf as . . . my patient's mother" (p. 130).

The central idea of the tragedy is, then, the deafness—and thus the guilt—of all men who prefer not to be aware of the world in which they live. For what Daniel tells his wife, in a cowardly effort to justify the police's role, is nonetheless true: "Mary, we live in terrible times. Those men are only executioners. If they're guilty, the whole society is guilty" (p. 34). And the words of the Police Commissioner Paulus likewise are correct when he states that society is responsible for what the police do to defend them, that the world is the same on the outside as it is at Headquarters, and that anybody is a fool to think that his work is done by a special breed of men. The attitude of crass indifference which characterizes society in general is underscored clearly by the gentleman in a tuxedo and the lady in

evening dress, who intervene in the play to advise the spectators
that the story they are about to see is merely entertainment:

GENTLEMAN: Yes, that's another thing we should make clear. If something like this happened, it didn't happen around here. If those
things take place at all, it's only in relatively uncivilized parts
of the world . . .
LADY: In some faraway country.
GENTLEMAN: So, as you see, you have no need to worry about it. The
story is probably false, and at any rate it comes to us from
distant lands and has absolutely nothing to do with us.
LADY: And above all, smile! There has always been a lot of misery
in the world, but by putting up with it we've learned to smile.
GENTLEMAN: And the smile is humanity's most beautiful accomplish-
ment. Take care of it.
LADY: Don't ever lose it. (p. 90)

Dr. Valmy tells us, when this couple appears near the end
of the play to warn against his incredible tale, that they were
his patients in his first case history, a knowledge of which is
essential to an understanding of the present one. After listening
to the doctor tell the second case history at the sanatorium, they
had called him a liar, even though they themselves were Daniel
and Mary's neighbors. The doctor was nevertheless forced to
release the couple the next day, for society does not consider
people mentally unbalanced merely because they will not admit
the truth. Nonetheless, Dr. Valmy implies, their skepticism is
actually madness.

After facing the truth about his past, Daniel continues his
struggle to redeem himself, asking for an indefinite leave of
absence from his position under the pretext that he is ill. As he
might have foreseen, however, the Commissioner denies his
request, and threatens, furthermore, to brand him as a traitor
and submit him to the same treatment he has inflicted on others.
Nevertheless, Daniel refuses to admit to himself or to his wife
the hopelessness of his situation, concealing from her his failure
in his effort to quit his job, rationalizing the necessity for work-
ing a few days longer in order to obtain eventual release, and
trying desperately to convince himself that the Commissioner
will at least permit him to transfer to service in a foreign country
where he can defect. "Somewhere," he tells Mary, "forgiveness

is waiting for me. It's up to me to find it and to deserve it" (p. 155). Mary points out that despite his search for the truth Daniel has not abandoned his self-deceptions. For neither Mary nor Lucila can forgive him, not to mention the latter's husband, who has died of heart failure during further interrogation—a fact Daniel has attempted to conceal from his wife. As Daniel himself admits in a moment of sincerity and lucidity, everything between Mary and him has been a lie.

Daniel's despair, however, drives him to a final confrontation with Paulus in which he summons courage to refuse to continue his work and to condemn the latter's ideology:

PAULUS: I didn't invent torture. When you and I came into the world, torture was already here. Just like pain and death. It may be a savage institution, but it's justified by the fact that we live among savages.

DANIEL: Justified. Against human beings?

PAULUS: Why the hell are you so worried about human beings? You've seen them in here: you know that most of them aren't worth spitting on. Don't you realize that every bit of progress man has ever achieved has involved innumerable crimes? (*A cry of pain is heard. Both look at the door.*)

DANIEL: You mean innumerable martyrs.

PAULUS: Don't be a fool! Of course every undertaking has had its martyrs, but it has also had its torturers.

DANIEL: Yes. And the torturers have putrified every movement they've ever been associated with. (p. 159)

The details of the political struggle or the supposed acts of sedition—whether by the right or left—explains Dr. Valmy, are purposely omitted from his case history in order that the fundamental questions posed may stand out more sharply. That the story is recent, however, is indicated by references to the launching of a space station. Each reader, the doctor explains, must take these questions, meditate on them, and see if he is honest enough not to avoid formulating answers.

When Paulus, no longer comfortable in Daniel's presence, unexpectedly indicates that he will let him transfer at an opportune moment, the latter finally dares to believe that he can be free, that he can once more resume a normal relationship with his wife. For Mary, however, it is too late. The truth about Daniel, so long resisted, has led to her insanity. Toward her

husband she feels only repulsion as she experiences a nightmare
in which she and their baby son are victims of his torture. Her
reaction to his pleas for her love and understanding and for a
chance to start all over again is to threaten him with a pistol in
the belief that he is about to harm their baby. "In a bond
between two people," as Dr. Valmy states, "a lie is a little worm
that can corrode the union. But sometimes, after the worm has
been there a while, it's better not to try to replace him with
the truth" (p. 135).

"Go on, go on back to them! You'll always go back to them,
won't you?" Mary asks Daniel. "Your boss knows you will, and
you know it, too! You'll go back because you want to!" (p. 168).
Daniel realizes at last that all his hopes were delusions, that
the doctor's words about the very high price he must pay are
true, that Paulus has deceived him, and that he will never get
well. There is, in short, no way out. It is, as Mary has said, as
if their relationship is "damned." Advancing toward his wife,
despite her warning screams he accepts his fate. As the shots
ring out, he embraces death as the only solution. The play,
comments Dr. Valmy, is the story of an insignificant person
who has to face an extraordinary situation, a person lacking
not in sensitivity, but courage—a courage few men would have
in his situation. The tragedy ends on an ironic note as the
Grandmother tells the baby the same story she once told his
father: "Once there was a little baby boy, pretty as sunshine,
and his name was Danny.... And Danny was handsome and
good ... and he had a mama who adored him.... And she
would say: 'My Danny is going to be big and strong like a
soldier.' And Danny would smile.... And she would say: 'He's
so good that everybody will want to be his friend,' and Danny
would smile..." (p. 169).

Daniel's defeat seems to affirm the conviction Mary expressed
earlier that all men are destined to become either victims or
executioners, and that her son's fate will be that of his father.
Life, she says, is not the beautiful, exhilarating thing she once
thought, but a filthy trap into which all men must fall. Hope
for the future, nevertheless, is seen in Daniel's words to Paulus
after the latter attempts to justify the use of torture. When the
Commissioner states that the reason it is not included in the
official book of regulations is that people are too childish

to understand its necessity, Daniel answers: "You're wrong. They're just beginning to understand. People used to put up with torture centuries ago, when they were more childish than they are now. Today torture is hidden. It's kept out of sight like a freak child. You sit there defending it, but I notice you do it in a low voice with the doors closed. In public you have to smile like a kindly old gentleman who loves his fellowman" (p. 160).

In *The Double Case History of Dr. Valmy,* as in the other four plays discussed in this chapter, we see man's search for the truth or "light" about his relationship with other individuals. In *The Awaited Sign,* Enrique tries to learn if his wife really loves him; in *Dawn,* Amalia attempts to ascertain her dead husband's attitude toward her; in *Today's a Holiday,* Silverio struggles to bridge the gap which separates him from his wife by confessing a past offense; and in *The Cards Face Down,* Juan strives to clarify his relationship with his entire family, to see the cards which they maintain face down. In *The Double Case History of Doctor Valmy,* Daniel consults a psychiatrist in a desperate attempt to ascertain the truth about his marriage. In the case of Silverio, Juan and Daniel, we see the protagonists' initial unwillingness to face the truth, their self-deceptions, and evasion. As the result of some crisis, however, all of these protagonists finally seek the light of understanding. In this, they differ from Asaf and Ulysses. Major themes in all five plays are man's blind incomprehension of himself and others, his isolation, and his inability to communicate on any meaningful level. In *Today's a Holiday* and *The Cards Face Down,* this lack of communication is represented scenically by Pilar's deafness and Anita's muteness. Buero uses these human limitations, just as he uses blindness in plays to be discussed later, on both the literal and symbolic planes.

In addition to the struggle to achieve meaningful interpersonal relationships, *Today's a Holiday, The Cards Face Down,* and, to a lesser degree, *The Double Case History of Dr. Valmy* depict the struggle to realize oneself through one's work. In these plays, we see man's struggle not only against the limitations, not only of his own personality, that is, his own blindness, but of social and economic circumstances. Like *Story of a Stairway,* the first play Buero had performed, which gave a new direction to the Spanish stage, *Today's a Holiday*, especially, exposes social realities of present-day Spaniards of humble social position: their poverty and suffering.

Even in this type of play, however, there lies under the surface an emphasis upon the metaphysical, which has its roots in everyday life. Through the visionary figure of Pilar, in *Today's a Holiday*, Buero manages to convey a sense of the mystery of life. She is the "link between the commonplace and the mysterious," one critic states.[33] "The insinuation of imponderable mysteries surrounding the action of the play," he continues, "has been one of the constants of Buero's dramatic art." Comments another critic: "Perhaps the most beautiful thing about *Today's a Holiday* is this combination, achieved with an innate mastery, of a lowly reality with an admirable poetic sense."[34]

With *The Double Case History of Dr. Valmy*, we enter into still another area of concern—the political—which will be more evident in Buero's historical plays to be discussed in a later chapter. Man's spiritual blindness, his indifference to the plight of his fellowmen, is represented, as we have seen, by the Grandmother's deafness. Here, as in all Buero's theater, we see the ethical emphasis of the playwright. Indeed, it has been stated that "authenticity in ethics and aesthetics would seem to be the key to Antonio Buero Vallejo's dramatic production."[35]

This group of plays, as the last, is illustrative of the variety of techniques which characterizes Buero's theater. The poetic and lyrical atmosphere of *The Awaited Sign* resembles that of *The Dream Weaver* and *Almost a Fairy Tale*. The remaining plays, particularly *Today's a Holiday* and *The Cards Face Down*, the first of which depicts lower-class and the second of which depicts middle-class or bourgeois Spanish society, are more in the tradition of social realism. The settings of these plays, especially the tenement house in the heart of Madrid in *Today's a Holiday*, are reminiscent of Galdós. *The Cards Face Down*, Buero himself remarks, is in the more or less direct tradition of Galdós and Ibsen.[36] In all these plays, Buero's "extraordinary capacity to extract from ordinary everyday life all in it that is [...] tragic" is evident.[37]

The realism in these plays, however, is much more than a reflection of external reality. It is realism of a symbolic sort.

Therefore, it would be a serious mistake rigidly to classify these tragedies as "realistic" in opposition to others such as *The Dream Weaver* and *Almost a Fairy Tale,* which are "symbolic" or "spiritual"—which is precisely what many critics have done. We have seen that Buero himself rejects any such divisions and prefers to speak of a "symbolic realism." In the plays in the group just discussed, as in all Buero's theater, external reality is endowed with symbolic, and often mysterious, meaning. These plays represent, as Vásquez Zamora states, "a tragic sense which is in the best Spanish tradition"—that of the transcendent realism of Galdós: "The fact is that Buero Vallejo is a dramatist who is radically Spanish, profoundly immersed in the tradition of Spanish transcendental realism and the influence of great foreign dramatists upon him is always in that line of affinities."[38]

Man's Struggle for Self-Realization: Will versus Aboulia

> "But you haven't freed yourself! You're still tied to this stairway, just like me and the rest of us."
> —*Historia de una escalera* (*Story of a Stairway*)[1]

WHEREAS the emphasis in the preceding plays is upon man's struggle to realize himself through creating meaningful human relationships, the emphasis in several other plays falls upon his efforts to fulfill himself through his work. These latter plays represent a search for the "light" or understanding which may enable him to accomplish something worthwhile, something to give meaning to life. The obstacles which the protagonist must overcome include social and economic limitations imposed by society as well as his personal limitations. The theme of self-fulfillment through constructive endeavor has been seen in *Today's a Holiday,* in which Silverio fails to fulfill his potential and abandons ambitions he once had to become an artist, and in *The Cards Face Down,* where Juan is unable to win a professorship. In the latter tragedy, moreover, we witness the characters' concern with the passage of time, which seems to accentuate man's failures—their references to their apartment's everwidening cracks and crumbling cornice. These themes, however, are secondary, for it is the characters' failure in the area of personal relationships which is largely responsible for their defeat. In three tragedies, however, these themes become paramount: *Historia de una escalera* (*Story of a Stairway*), 1949, *El tragaluz* (*The Basement Window*), 1967, and *Concert at Saint Ovide,* 1962.

I Historia de una escalera (Story of a Stairway)

In *Story of a Stairway,* as in most of Buero's tragedies, we see man torn between his limitations and his dreams of self-fulfillment. Fernando and Urbano, inhabitants of a working-class tenement house, long to "rise" above the sordidness of their existence. Fernando, a young clerk, longs for a brilliant career as an engineer. His hopes for happiness are seen in his conversation with Carmina, a young girl who lives in the same house:

FERNANDO: Starting tomorrow I'm going to work hard for you. I want to get out of this poverty, this sordid atmosphere . . . To end this anguish of not having enough money . . . I'm going to study a lot . . . First, I'll become a draftsman . . . I'll study to be a rigger next. By then you'll be my wife, and we'll live in another neighborhood, in an apartment that's clean and quiet. I'll keep on studying . . . And maybe by then I'll become an engineer . . .

CARMINA: We'll be so happy! (p. 33)

Fernando, however, never even begins this career of which he dreams and, even though he still loves Carmina, finally marries another neighbor, Elvira, for her father's money.

Urbano, a worker who inhabits the same building, also has dreams of advancement which are never fulfilled. These dreams are shown in his words to Carmina, who finally marries him after the death of her father, although she is not in love with him: "If you accept me, I'll get ahead. Yes, I'll get ahead. Because when I have you at my side, I'll have the energy to work. To work for you! I'll become a better mechanic and I'll earn more" (p. 45).

Fernando's and Urbano's hopes and failures are seen against the background of the unhappiness and poverty of four families which occupy adjacent apartments. In each of the three acts of the tragedy, the characters' lives are shown at a successive period: 1919, 1929, and 1949. In the course of these years, most of the old generation die and are replaced by a third generation, children of the central characters, who have the same hopes as their parents once had. As in *Today's a Holiday,* many of the characters who live together in the apartment house are popular types found in the Spanish sainete or brief farce: for example, the light man, Paca, "the loud-mouthed neighbor with a heart of gold," and doña Asunción, the pretentious woman who spends beyond her means.[2] We witness the neighbors' joys and sorrows, their dreams and illusions, their love affairs, marriages, and

funeral processions. As Marquerie states, the play is in the
magnificent tradition of realism and *costumbrismo* (criticism of
manners and customs) in the Spanish theater, which starts with
the classics and continues with Galdós and Dicenta[3]—although
other critics have seen an affinity with North American playwrights such as O'Neill, Wilder, and Elmer Rice.[4] Buero himself states that he attempted, under the surface of a farcelike
criticism of customs and manners, to depict an authentic tragedy.[5]

The importance of the role of time in the tragedy is emphasized
by the setting, the stairway where the tenants meet. As the years
pass, it remains practically the same,, "worn and dirty," reminding
them of their hopes and failures of the changelessness of their
lives. "How old I am!" exclaims doña Paca, in a lengthy monologue, "as old as you." The neighbors' anguish at the passage of
time is perhaps most clearly expressed in Fernando's speech in
the first act:

> That's not what bothers me, Urbano. The fact is that I'm afraid
> of time. That's what makes me suffer most. Just seeing the days and
> the years pass . . . without anything ever changing. Only yesterday
> you and I were two kids who came here to hide and smoke our first
> cigarettes. . . . And that was ten years ago! We've grown up without
> realizing it, going up and down the stairs, surrounded by parents
> who don't understand us, neighbors who gossip about us and about
> whom we gossip. . . . Resorting to a thousand tricks and putting
> up with humiliations to pay the rent, the electricity . . . and potatoes.
> (*A pause.*) And tomorrow or ten years from now, which can go by
> like one day, like the last couple of years. . . . It would be awful
> to go on like this! Going up and down the stairway, a stairway
> leading nowhere; cheating on the meters, hating work . . . losing
> one day after another . . . (*Pause.*) That's why we have to act once
> and for all. (pp. 21-22)

Arturo del Hoyo aptly describes this tragedy, which spans thirty
years, as the dramatization of the totality of man's existence
rather than a partial aspect of it, and states that the play's "tragic
sense" comes precisely from "the uneventfulness of life, the
obvious uneventfulness of the stairway, the identity of the seg-
ments of existence," that is, the changelessness that remains
man's fate.[6] Buero comments that he was particularly concerned
with time and space as limitations to man's self-realization, upon
writing the play.[7] These limitations are represented by the stair-

way, including its two landings, where the entire action of the play takes place. Buero's technical skill here, as in *Today's a Holiday*, where all the events occur on a tenement rooftop, has been highly praised by critics who have spoken of his 'theatrical carpentry or architecture." Marquerie notes the "sobriety" which comes from the compactness of plot, the lack of spectacular visual effects, and the way in which the characters' presence on the stairway is justified at each moment,[8] while del Hoyo states that the tragedy produces the impression of "a being with a backbone, which hides a substantial marrow."[9]

If the stairway, as we have seen, represents the obstacles of time and of space, that is, of economic and social environment, it is obvious that it in itself does not cause the characters' defeat. It is merely the dimension in which the consequences of their own lack of action and decision are manifested. It is the characters' blindness to their own deficiencies which is responsible for their failure to overcome the obstacles or limitations symbolized by the stairway. The plans of both Fernando and Urbano are seen in a dialogue in the first act. Whereas Urbano had pinned his hopes for achieving a better standard of living on the union and collective action, Fernando had relied only upon himself:

URBANO: Fernando, you're a poor wretch, and the worst part of it is that you don't know it. Poor devils like us will never attain a better life without helping each other. That's what the union stands for. Solidarity! That's our motto. And it would be yours if you'd realize that you're only a poor clerk, not the marquis you think you are.

FERNANDO: I don't think I'm anything. I just want to get ahead. Do you understand? Get ahead! And escape all this sordidness we live in.

URBANO: And the hell with everyone else.

FERNANDO: Why should I care about others? No one does anything for anybody. You join the union because you can't get ahead by yourself. But that's not the way for me. I know that I can get ahead alone and I will. (pp. 19-20)

The failure of both is seen in their words in the last act. "And what's happened to all your plans for work?" Urbano asks Fernando. "All you've ever done is look over the other guy's shoulder. But you haven't freed yourself! (*Striking the handrail.*)

You're still tied to this stairway, just like me and the rest of us."
Fernando, in turn, replies: "Yes, just like you. You, too, were
going to go far with your union and your solidarity. (*Ironically.*)
You were going to fix things for everybody... even for me"
(pp. 69-70).

Fernando fails because he spends his time in bed reading,
planning, and writing poetry, always intending to work "starting
tomorrow." He is the dreamer without the willpower to develop
his potential. Therefore he is defeated by his circumstances. His
cowardice in marrying Elvira for her money, moreover, is the
cause of the unhappiness of Carmina whom he loves, but who
finally marries Urbano, although she does not love him, when he
offers to protect her after her father's death. Urbano, who unlike
Fernando, is a good and hard-working man, has few dreams. His
failure comes from his lack of self-confidence. "I know I'm just
a poor worker," he tells Carmina. "I don't have any culture and I
can't aspire to be anything important.... It's better that way. At
least I won't have to suffer deceptions like others suffer" (p. 45).

In an article entitled *"Historia de una escalera*: A Play in
Search of Characters," Robert Kirsner observes that the characters
"do not act out the roles that they have assigned to themselves.
It is as though they were struck down before they could begin
their drama. Incapable of sustaining dreams, they disintegrate
before they can do battle."[10] He adds that the epigraph from
Micah (7:6) thus seems ironic for we are led to expect that the
characters will rise up or rebel against their progenitors, but this
does not happen.

In an article in *Renascence*, David Foster comments that "the
roots of Fernando's and Urbano's failure lie, really, not in the
incapacity of the human individual ever to dominate his existence, but rather in a personal ineptness and lack of desire to do
so—in short, in aboulia."[11] Expanding on Valbuena Prat's statement (in *Historia de la literatura española*, III, Barcelona, 1960,
845), that the play embodies Ortega y Gasset's "the theme of our
time becomes existential, all that is agonal diffused throughout
the story, but always implacable or impassive," Foster states that
Story of a Stairway "thematically (and in its stark simplicity,
artistically) seems a work of the Generation of 1898, which
introduced the companion themes of aboulia and a new spontaneous vitality into Spanish literature. Pío Baroja's anti-heroes

un-motivated by a lack of will, are answered by Miguel de Unamuno's characters whose calculated will power and frightening intense vitality are often their only personality traits. [. . .] It is within this sphere of influence that *Historia de una escalera* moves."

The tragedy ends as Fernando, Jr. tells the younger Carmina of his dreams for the future in almost the same words that his father used thirty years ago. Their parents, who overhear them, gaze at each other with an infinite melancholy across the stairwell as they experience the return of the past in a scene quite reminiscent of Azorín.

FERNANDO, JR.: We've got to be stronger than our parents were. They let life get the better of them. They've spent thirty years going up and down these stairs . . . each day getting more miserly and common. But we won't let this place defeat us. No! We'll leave here. . . . There's only brutality and misunderstanding for us here. Listen to me. If I know that you'll go on loving me, I'll accomplish many things. First I'll become a rigger. It's not so hard. In a couple of years I'll be a good one. I'll earn a lot of money and all the building contractors will want me. By that time we'll be married. . . . We'll have our own happy, clean home, far from here. But I won't stop studying just for that. No, Carmina. Next I'll become an engineer. I'll be the best engineer in the country and you'll be my darling wife. (pp. 74-75)

Although Foster, in the article mentioned above, considers that Fernando, Jr. seems to possess the "spontaneous vitality" necessary to succeed, the ending seems more ambivalent. Of course it does not close the door on hope. Repetition by the children of their parents' mistakes is a grave probability given the environment in which they have grown up. Nevertheless we know that, for Buero, adverse destiny is a danger which arises from man's blindness and self-deception, but it is never a certainty. The playwright himself has commented: "The 'echo' of the parents' words in their children does not prejudge anything. It is the vague warning that the repetition of human events sometimes affords us. Perhaps the children will escape their elders' mistakes or—perhaps—they, too, will fail."[12] The playwright himself does not know.

II El tragaluz (The Basement Window)

In its depiction of social and economic immobility, *The Basement Window* is similar to *Story of a Stairway*. Here, however, present-day society is examined by two enlightened beings of another century. The play is the historical tragedy of a family destroyed by the Spanish Civil War and forced to take refuge in a squalid basement apartment from which they have been unable to escape. The work is narrated by investigators living at a future time, whose scientific progress allows them to look back and detect images of the past mysteriously preserved in space. The narrators appear on stage to indicate, very significantly, that the tragedy which they have reconstructed is a collective one, that the family depicted represents merely one out of many. It is the story "of a few trees, now dead, within an immense forest."[13]

We learn from the investigators that this particular family missed the train which was to have taken them back to Madrid at the end of the war. Only the eldest son, Vicente, was able to board the train full of soldiers returning home. Since Vicente was carrying the family's provisions, his father ordered him to get off. However, he resisted and continued on the train alone to Madrid. The rest of the family was delayed six days, during which time the baby sister, Elvirita, died from lack of milk and was buried in one of the towns through which they passed. Once in Madrid, the father, mother, and younger son Mario, found shelter in the basement apartment where they have spent years of economic privation. Mario's description of himself as "a man broken since the end of our war" aptly characterizes the entire family except Vicente, who has left home. Thus we see that the basement apartment represents "the place of those who were left in the gutter."[14]

The basement suggests, further, a place of darkness and evasion, a refuge from the light of truth—the truth about what happened thirty years ago.[15] For the family has invented a fictitious version of the events, according to which Vicente was prevented from getting off the train by the jostling mob of soldiers. He is thus absolved of all responsibility. Although none of the family actually believes this version, they pretend to in order to make life bearable.

The old father has found in madness a refuge from the truth

of his daughter's death. He has spent his time in the basement apartment cutting out human figures from old post cards and watching the legs of the people who pass the open basement window—just as his children used to years ago, pretending they were in a theater. Now the father mysteriously insists that the window is a train window. Moreover, about all the figures outside the window and on the post cards, as well as about his two sons, he raises the same insistent question: "Who is that?" This query is the almost childish question of a madman. However, as the critic A. Fernández-Santos points out, in an article published in *Primer Acto*, "employed as an interrogation of all that exists, projected as a reexamination of reality which lies between the lyrical and the ironic, it becomes a strange sort of disconcerting truth."[16] The enigma of human identity is, of course, an important theme of Kierkegaard, Unamuno, and Beckett. In his article Fernández-Santos compares the father in Buero's play to the old madman of Beckett's *Krappe's Last Tape* who is absorbed by this same enigma. Concerning madness, Buero himself points that "in the realm of poetry the abnormal and unusual affords us a new access to reality or a new form of understanding."[17]

Like the father, Mario is, in the practical sense, a failure. Unable even to start his studies for the *bachillerato* or high school diploma at the end of the war because of the necessity of supporting the family, he has continued to read voraciously while doing odd jobs from time to time. Apparently lacking willpower and self-confidence, he chooses to remain in the basement as life passes him by. Vicente describes Mario's situation well when he admonishes him, "You are consuming your life here, while you observe an alienated man or spy through the skylight at the legs of insignificant people. You are dreaming! Wake up!" (p. 52).

In effect, Mario is the dreamer, the contemplative, who, echoing the father's question "Who is that?" longs to transcend the limits of human understanding. His questioning represents a search for the truth or understanding which will enable him to penetrate the enigma of man and his identity even though his reason tells him that this is impossible. He acknowledges that his dream of a vast investigation to discover the identity of persons pictured on old post cards is as foolish as wishing to ascertain the behavior of an electron in a distant galaxy. To Vicente's statement that his dream implies the point of view of God he confesses that it

is a point of view to which we will never attain but for which
we will always long. Vicente considers that Mario, who sees
reason and logic in his father's actions, is as mad as the latter. For
he looks through skylights and sees giants instead of windmills.
Nevertheless, as Buero himself comments, madness may result
in profoundly lucid intuitions to which ordinary reason cannot
attain. Buero adds that, when explicated by Mario, the father's
apparently incoherent question actually becomes an attempted
theory of reality.[18]

Vicente, the brother who left the family years ago and who
has achieved a high position in a publishing house, represents the
direct antithesis of Mario, the dreamer or idealist—he is the
practical man of action. This contrast is most clearly seen in
two confrontations during Vicente's visits to his parents' apartment. In the first, Mario explains his reasons for rejecting Vicente's
offer of a job with his company. Unlike Fernando and Urbano in
Story of a Stairway, he deliberately chooses poverty and
obscurity:

MARIO: (*He points to the father.*) Look at him. This poor old de-
mented man used to be an upright human being. Do you
remember? And he inculcated in us the religion of rectitude.
A dangerous lesson because [...] people don't live by rectitude
in our time.... People live by deceit, treachery, compromise.
... They live by trampling on others. What do you do then?
You either accept this sinister game ... and climb out of this
hole ... , or you remain in it.
VICENTE: Why not just get out?
MARIO: (*Coldly.*) That's what I'm trying to explain.... I despise
this life. [...] Its only rule is eat or be eaten. And on top of
that, everyone tells you: devour them before they devour
you! We'll give you pretty theories for your peace of mind.
The struggle for survival.... The end justifies the means....
Charity begins at home.... But from here, from my hole,
I'm trying to see if I can save myself from being devoured ...
without devouring. (pp. 50-51)

Vicente, the man of action, lacks Mario's ethical scruples.
The following exchange is occasioned by Vicente's willingness to
sacrifice the popular writer, Beltrán, to a new group of men who
impose their political ideas on the publishing house in exchange

for providing funds. The conversation clearly unmasks Vicente as
an egoist and opportunist.

VICENTE: What does it matter? We use their money, that's all.
MARIO: And they, don't they use you?
VICENTE: It's a necessary game. You don't understand it.
MARIO: Of course I understand the game. One becomes a bit of a
revolutionary, then a bit of a conservative. [...] The new group
exploits us.... We let ourselves be exploited because we
exploit them ... and everyone prospers. Who knows the games
people play today! Only the poor know what they are: poor.
[..]
VICENTE: There are reasons for all that.
MARIO: There are always reasons for being underhanded. (pp. 74-75)

The cynical Vicente is, thus, much the same type of egoistic
"reasoner" as Ulysses.

In his desire for power, Vicente, the egoist, destroys the one
man whom Mario idealizes precisely because he has gotten
ahead without compromising his integrity. Furthermore, he has
victimized his secretary, Encarna, a poor young countrygirl
orphaned shortly after her father came to the city to seek work.
Uneducated and inexperienced, she maintains her present position
only because she is Vicente's mistress. She is expecting his baby,
but is afraid to tell him lest he reject the child.

It is Mario's desire to force Vicente to face the truth about
himself, as well as their unconscious rivalry over Encarna, that
leads to the scene in which the former accuses his brother of
responsibility for his father's madness. The investigators state that
truth is always preferable to falsehood, even though it may prove
painful and even though it may lead only to further questions.
In this "trial," Mario accuses Vicente not only of having caused
the death of his baby sister, Elvirita, and the madness of his
father, but of having victimized and oppressed others ever since.
It is for the latter that Mario condemns him most harshly. The
war, Mario acknowledges, had been atrocious for everyone and
the future uncertain. Vicente suddenly understood that the sack
of provisions was his first booty. Both brothers grew up in
difficult times. Mario does not condemn Vicente because he was
merely a hungry and frightened child. However, as an adult, he
is guilty, in Mario's eyes. For he has continued to make victims.

When the train pulled away from the station, it carried away Vicente forever. He never got off.

With this accusation, Mario hopes to save his brother. It is obvious to him that Vicente himself seeks this confrontation with his conscience, as he returns more and more frequently to the apartment in an unconscious search for pardon. José María de Quinto remarks that guilt and punishment are essential to tragedy and that Vicente's increasingly frequent visits to the basement apartment—to that which is most profoundly authentic within himself—evince an unexpressed desire to assume responsibility for his actions.[19]

Vicente, alone with his father, confesses that he deliberately fought to remain aboard the train. Although he considers his father incapable of understanding him, Vicente confesses his guilt as if addressing a God in whom he does not believe, but for whom he ardently longs: "But He is not here, and no one is punished, and life goes on. Look at me; I'm weeping. In a minute I'll leave, with the illusion that you have heard me, to continue to create victims. . . . From time to time I'll reflect that I did all I could by confessing to you and that it was too late, since you don't understand. . . . The other madman, my brother, would tell me it is never too late. But who can put an end to vileness in a vile world?" (p. 98).

Vicente starts to leave the apartment—to "return to the train that never stops." However, the father, reliving the past, believes that his son is once again about to board the real train which took him away years ago. As the sound of the locomotive (heard whenever the characters look out of the basement window) becomes deafening the father, in a burst of madness—or of sanity— stabs Vicente repeatedly with the scissors until the noise slowly subsides and the stage lights fade out. Ricardo Doménech comments that Vicente's murder is both the crime of a madman and the tragic fulfillment of an ancient Dike or goddess of justice.[20] Mario's accusation thus leads to results which he has foreseen perhaps only subconsciously. He now understands that he himself is partially responsible for Vicente's death and that the latter really wished to pay for his mistakes: "He wanted to deceive himself . . . and to see clearly; I wanted to save him . . . and to kill him. What did we really want? . . . Who was the victim and who the executioner?" (p. 102).[21]

With the death of Vicente, the symbolism of the basement window becomes clear. The light which shines through it represents the truth about the past: Vicente's departure on the train, leaving his sister to die, and his subsequent refusal to get off.[22] The physical setting of the play is suggestive of the cave in Plato's allegory; and the flight, return, and death of one of the captives parallels Vicente's. However, whereas Plato's characters are incapable of imagining the light of reality outside, the inhabitants of Buero's basement are unable to escape it.[23] The past inexorably dominates the present. The figure of the father, like that of the basement window, is endowed with both real and allegorical significance.[24] Ambiguous and mysterious, he is both a pitiable madman and an all-knowing judge.

The entire play obviously represents a judgment—not merely upon Vicente (and Mario)—but upon an entire generation. The investigators, He and She, are absolutely essential to understanding the playwright's message, for their words make clear the historical dimension of the play: "The world was full of injustice, war, and fear. The activists forgot to contemplate; and those who contemplated didn't know how to act" (p. 100). Buero thus makes it clear that Mario, the contemplative or dreamer, is not without blame. "All action is impure," Vicente has stated. "But not everyone is an egoist. [...] You won't do anything useful if you do not act" (p. 52).

It is significant that the judgment which the play implies is made from the perspective of a future in which the hopes that Mario and Encarna express for Vicente's child, whom the latter bears and whom Mario has agreed to protect after their marriage, have been realized—a future in which the blindness and incomprehension which the play depicts have been overcome. "Today we no longer fall into those errors," state the investigators. This new world which Buero believes the man of the future will construct, putting his technology at the service of human need, is one "where it is not necessary to devour or to be devoured; where it is not necessary to say, as the mother says, 'cursed be men who start wars,' because there will be no wars; where man, every man will recognize himself in others."[25] Through the two investigators from the future, Buero thus expresses his faith in the better, more just society which Vicente's generation has felt impotent to build, and thus imparts to the spectator a sense of hope for the future.

Even more importantly, however, the investigators (although they speak from a future age) involve the spectator with the present, disconcerting and disquieting him. Rather than detracting from the play's relevancy or mitigating its effect upon today's audience, the narrators intensify its impact, forcing the spectator to feel himself and his society as objects of judgment.

The investigators' main purpose, Buero comments, is to "move the public," thus making it clear that although they clarify rationally many aspects of the play, they are not intended as a Brechtian device.[26] Their function is to make the spectator not only understand rationally, but, more importantly, feel emotively how his actions may some day be discovered and implacably judged. In other words, the investigators bring about on the part of the viewer not only reflection, but a type of fear:[27] "If you haven't *felt*, at some moment," states one of the investigators toward the end of the work, "like true creatures of the twentieth century, but observed and judged by a sort of future conscience; if you haven't *felt*, at some moment, like beings from a future already become present, who judge, with rigor and pity, very ancient people, perhaps just like you, the experiment has failed" (p. 100 [Italics added]). In effect, the future becomes present as the play functions as a "test" or "trial" of the spectator's own painful and often repressed memories of the civil war period. The importance of this "test" is seen in the words of one of the investigators: "Assuming the past makes our advance slower, but, also, firmer" (p. 83).

It is significant that Buero states that he sees signs, now for the first time, of Spanish society's, willingly or unwillingly, acquiring an awareness of its problems. Doménech summarizes the message of the play when he remarks that man must assume his role and commit himself. He continues that this can only be done from a position of moral rectitude and through the creation of a collective social conscience.[28]

For, in effect, the guilt of Vicente and Mario is the spectators'. "We know now that we are one," states the feminine narrator, "not only with those who live now, but with the entire past. Innocent with those who were innocent and guilty with those who were guilty" (p. 82). To the query, "Who is that?" be it the father's question as he refers to figures who pass by the basement window or the investigators' question as they observe the subjects of their experiment—the answer is, in a certain sense, that given by She as she addresses the spectators: "That one is you, and you, and you. I am you, and you are me. All of us have lived and all will live all lives. If all persons had thought, when they wounded and tortured others that they themselves were the ones who suffered, they wouldn't have done it. . . . Let us think of it in this way until the real answer arrives" (p. 83). The collective tragedy of Spanish society, *The Basement Window*, is thus, no less, the individual tragedy of man as an ontological enigma. The play develops from a portrayal of contemporary Spain and her problems into an anguished inquiry into the human condition, into the mystery of man and of existence itself. Both social and metaphysical in scope, it is, in the narrators' words, "an experiment in total reality."

III El concierto de San Ovidio (The Concert at Saint Ovide)

Whereas the characters in *Story of a Stairway* and *The Basement Window* must face the limitation of spiritual blindness to, or incomprehension of, their personal deficiencies. David, the protagonist of *The Concert at Saint Ovide*, is physically blind. However, his physical blindness and the unenlightened attitude of society which forces him to beg in the streets are meant to represent any external limitation or barrier to self-realization. Since blindness is, also, a lack of vision and to conquer it, even partially, is to discover a facet of truth, David's explicit search for "light" symbolizes any man's struggle for the knowledge or understanding which will permit him to overcome his limitations. It is obvious, therefore, that the play does not deal only with the blind. David's struggle represents the conflict between "liberty" or free will and "necessity" with which, in Buero's view, all tragedy deals. In the playwright's own words, his efforts constitute "a sane rebellion against our limitations which plants the possibility of overcoming them."[29]

David's desire for self-fulfillment is expressed semipoetically when he speaks of Melania de Salignac, the blind lady who can read and write both books and music, and with whose image he is secretly in love.[30] Just as Don Quijote dreams of Dulcinea,

100 ANTONIO BUERO VALLEJO

the symbol of the ideal, David, the blind beggar, dreams of Melania, especially when he plays on his violin the "Adagio" from Corelli's "Concerto Grosso in G Minor." This music, repeated several times throughout the tragedy, becomes representative of his yearnings: "I speak to her and I play for her! And I look for her. I look for that blind woman . . . who would understand . . ."[31] As one critic has stated, Melania represents, for David, a symbol "of what he can become . . . of liberty and of the possibilities of man."[32]

David, a beggar of the Asylum of the Quinze-Vingts in Paris in 1771, who plays the violin in the streets and who has innate talent, dreams of becoming a real musician. This represents, for him, a means of overcoming his blindness, of reaching the "light." It becomes, therefore, the object of all his striving: "I must play." When Valindin, an impresario, offers to hire David and five other blind beggars from the Asylum to play during the fair of Saint Ovide, David hopes passionately that he and his companions may learn to become real musicians and thus overcome their degradation. David, a man of infinite faith and willpower, believes that he and his companions can learn to harmonize even though they cannot read the score. For David, "it's just a matter of wanting it," as we see in his efforts to persuade his companions to follow him!

DAVID: But you have to want to! You have to say yes to your violin!
DONATO: (*Rises.*) All right, I'll say it!
DAVID: Thank you, Donato. (*He gropingly takes his hand.*)
LUCAS: (*Bitterly.*) You're just a blind man swinging wildly about with his cane!
DAVID: (*He feverishly draws back his hand and strikes the floor with his stick.*) A blind man's blows can be as deadly as anyone else's arrows! You think I'm deluded because I talk to you about Melania! But Nazario, you know that with my stick I can hit you right on the back of the neck whenever I want to! I've done it many times when we were playing. And you know why? Because when I was a boy, they laughed at me when I tried to use my stick to defend myself against bullies! I decided my stick was going to become an eye, and that's just what it is. Brothers, if we all decide that our violins are going to sing together, they will! It's just a matter of *wanting* it! And if you don't want it, just resign yourself to this living death that has us trapped here. (*A silence.*) (p. 16)

Not all the beggars, however, share David's longings, for they are resigned to their limitations. "Won't you ever stop dreaming?" David's companions ask him. To this the dreamer replies: "You're all dead and don't even know it! You're all cowards!" Nazario, especially, whose only desire is "eating and screwing," represents the man who refuses to confront the reality of his situation, preferring to forget or adapt to his limitations. David, however, cannot understand this type of fiction, of hypocrisy, of "joyful negation of reality."[33] He refuses to accept a blindness which he feels "God cannot have wanted." This opposition between David and Nazario, between the dreamer and the man whose rationalism has led to skepticism and fatalism, is not fully developed, however, for it is Valindin who is David's antagonist.

David rebels against not only his blindness, but the attitude of others toward his problem. He protests the egoism, the seemingly insuperable evil of a society which looks upon the blind as objects of diversion. "The people who have eyes," he tells Nazario, "must be convinced that we are men like they are—not sick little animals!" (p. 15). Valindin, it turns out, has no intention of having the beggars taught even an elementary harmony. He wants only to use them as a circus number, to convert them into clowns. Under the guise of philanthropy, Valindin, the "reasoner" interested only in making money, takes advantage of the beggars to exploit and humiliate them: "I'm good-hearted and philanthropic," he tells his mistress Adriana, "but remember, my dear, that philanthropy is also profitable. Those blind men are going to bring in money for us, and I'll pay them by teaching them to live! At the Asylum they were rotting away, little by little. With me they're going to become famous, and they'll be able to earn a living for themselves . . . (*His voice chokes.*) It's so elevating to do good for one's fellowman!" (pp. 18-19).

In *The Concert at Saint Ovide,* we have the same pessimistic vision of society as divided into exploiters and the exploited that Mario holds, in *The Basement Window,* as the result of his brother's egoism. Valindin represents the same type of egoistic "reasoner," interested only in promoting his own welfare, as Vicente or Ulysses in *The Dream Weaver.* The greater dramatic impact of the present play comes from the fact that the exploited are blind. "In effect," writes Laín Entralgo, "it happens that

the world is physically and morally opaque; if its physical
opaqueness can be overcome with ingenuity, which is so often
capable of illuminating caverns and abysses or of divining
invisible structures, the moral opaqueness of the world—egoism
and cruelty are its most common names—frequently resists."[34]

Buero's play is based on a historical event, even though the
characters are invented, with the exception of Valindin, whose
existence is historical, and Valentín Haüy, who appears later in
the play. In 1771, at the annual fair of Saint Ovide, an unscrupulous innkeeper had a group of blind beggars from the Asylum
give a burlesque concert dressed in dunces' caps, asses' ears,
and huge pasteboard spectacles. Buero reproduces this concert
in a scene based on an engraving from the period. His esperpentesque concert, with brilliantly colored robes, an enormous
painted peacock, the symbol of stupidity, and the grotesque
gestures of the blind beggars as they produce a music of mechanical precision but no feeling, evinces an ability to create plastic
effects which will be seen in several of the plays not yet
discussed.

David struggles unsuccessfully until the end, both to convince
his complacent companions that his dreams are possible and
to force Valindin to permit him to attempt to realize them. Like
Penelope in *The Dream Weaver* and Mario in *The Basement
Window*, David represents the dreamer or idealist. However,
whereas Mario is content to contemplate life as it passes by
the basement window, David strives to put his dreams into
action. Like his namesake, that other musician, the biblical
David, he is a rebel. Both dreams and action are necessary in
Buero's poetic world for, without dreams, the man of action like
Vicente becomes corrupt and "takes the train" the wrong way
and, without action, the contemplative like Mario remains
paralyzed. A man of tremendous willpower, a "man of action,
a born agitator," as one critic describes him,[35] David rebels
against the "darkness" to reach the light; and his rebellion
represents the struggle with which all of Buero's tragedies deal:
that against the "darkness" imposed by one's own deficiencies,
by society, or by an inscrutable Destiny. In his struggle, the
rebellious dreamer brings not peace, but strife to his companions
who lack his willpower and immense faith. A solitary figure,
he is understood only by Adriana, Valindin's mistress, who her-

self has suffered much. In her David finds a woman of flesh and blood to take the place of the unreal Melania. Indeed, David's struggle against Valindin is intensified and made more credible by their rivalry over Adriana, just as Mario's hatred of Vicente results, in part, from his love for Encarna, whom his brother has exploited.

David's rebellion culminates in the murder of Valindin, after the latter has prevented him from becoming the musician he could have been, had threatened to imprison him with a *lettre de cachet*, and beaten Adriana. Going at night to the café where Valindin is alone, after extinguishing the lantern, he kills the impresario with his cane in a masterful scene which takes place in total darkness. As the result of this crime, David, betrayed by his friend and fellow beggar Donato who is jealous of Adriana, is hanged. The tragedy, which Buero aptly subtitled a parable, ends with the betrayal and death of the dreamer who strives to find the "light" and to guide others to it. Against the egoism of society, the idealism of the dreamer seems powerless.

David's dreams, nevertheless, do continue to live on in the people whom he has influenced: in Adriana, in Donato, who years later walks alone through the streets playing only Corelli's "Adagio," and especially in Valentín Haüy, who, moved by the sad spectacle of the beggars' grotesque concert which he has witnessed, devotes his life to devising systems to enable the blind to read. Historically, Haüy, an inventor of a type of braille and founder of a school for the blind, was among those who witnessed the concert by the beggars from the Asylum in 1771. In words taken from one of his letters, Buero has him declare: "I'll make this ridiculous farce come true. I'll teach the blind to read. . . . I'll place in their hands books which they themselves have printed. I'll teach them to trace out the letters and then read their own writing. And I'll teach them to play beautiful music!" (p. 61). Haüy appears again, as an old man, in the last scene of Buero's tragedy, and reminisces about the events which led to David's death and their result. "When I saw those poor wretches subjected to such humiliation, I realized that my own life had a meaning. At the time I was unheard of: Valentin Haüy, linguist and music-lover. A nobody. But the most obscure individual in the world can do wonders if he so desires" (p. 61).

David's dreams have in this way come true. The tragic events which the "optimistic" tragedy has depicted have thus resulted in man's reaching the "light." They have led to man's triumph over one of his limitations. The illuminating lesson of the play has been summarized as follows: "In the face of the intractable attitude expressed by those who say that the world is unchangeable, that nothing can be altered, that one must be resigned, we, like David, must offer the opposing view that the world is not unchangeable, that everything can be altered, that man must not resign himself to his destiny, that the possibilities of man are unlimited, that Melania de Salignac does exist."[36]

David's struggle to become a musician in *The Concert at Saint Ovide* represents the same search for the "light" or understanding necessary to self-realization through the triumph over social and economic limitations as *Story of a Stairway*, in which Fernando longs to become an engineer, and *The Basement Window*, in which Mario abandons all ambition while Vicente achieves success in a publishing house by exploiting others. All three plays show the concern for the poor, defenseless, and abandoned that is a major characteristic of Buero's theater, and which we have seen in *Today's a Holiday*. We see their frustrated illusions, sorrows, and misery in an injust society. Of course, their failures stem, partially, from their own lack of character, particularly in *Story of a Stairway*. Nevertheless, what is condemned most strongly is their exploitation by unscrupulous opportunists such as Vicente and Valindin. García Pavón states that, for its social and moral intent, *The Concert at Saint Ovide* is "an almost gospel-like and irrefutable work." The same may be said of Buero's theater in general.[37]

A means of creating a better society, the society of which Mario dreams as he contemplates the bestial struggle in the world outside in *The Basement Window*, would seem to be the change in ethical attitudes of which the narrators speak in the same play and upon which Buero expresses his faith that a new, more just society will be constructed in a future age. The play is a defense of idealism and self-denial—the "religion of rectitude" which Mario says the old father taught his sons. José María de Quinto points out that the ethical attitudes indicated by the narrators are, in general, derived from existentialist or Christian theory.[38] In an article in *Razón y Fe*, another critic examines the narrators' answer to the father's question "Who is that?"— "That one is you, and you, and you," etc., in which they advocate each man putting himself in the other's place. They advance a concept of mutual solidarity and interdependence which unites each man with his brothers, the past with the future.[39]

When asked to define "social theater" in an interview published in *Arriba*, Buero responds as follows: "For me it is not only that [theater] which shows conflicts and problems of the most dispossessed classes as they are related to the imperfect structures of society, but also that [theater] which approaches any human problematic which has its origin in, or is associated with, these imperfect structures. In this sense, I believe that diverse forms of historical and political theater, as well as some philosophical and psychological [theater] lie within this concept."[40] He adds that its purpose is "emotive and reflective, oriented toward a positive transformation of society," although as we have seen, he also considers all tragedy as an instrument of perception and knowledge of reality, and not only transformation, involving active contemplation.

Many of Buero's plays portray directly present-day Spanish lower- and middle-class society: *Today's a Holiday, The Cards Face Down, Story of a Stairway,* and *The Basement Window.* Termed "tragedies of ordinary life" by José María de Quinto, they depict the anguish and despair of the poor and oppressed, often through profound psychological studies of character.[41] De Quinto considers Buero a "neogaldosian" author who paints the same sad and wretched Madrid inhabited by Spaniards of humble social position as Benito Pérez Galdós, whom he calls "the author most involved with his milieu which the contemporary Spanish literary world has produced." This Madrid is that of the terrace rooftops, stairways, and squalid apartments of *Today's a Holiday, Story of a Stairway,* and *The Basement Window.*

As we see in Buero's definition of "social theater" given above, however, the social is not limited to those plays which focus directly upon the reality of contemporary society, but includes works such as *The Concert at Saint Ovide,* which depict the tragedy of present-day Spanish society—its servitude and degradation—under the guise of treating a historical situation. Buero's other historical tragedies will be discussed in the following chapter.

Those plays which testify directly to contemporary Spanish life, with the exception of *The Basement Window* (1967), were written early in Buero's career. They develop in the Ibsen manner around psychological motives. They are generally characterized by a "closed form" in which the unities are carefully observed—especially that of place, which is used symbolically. The stairway and the terrace rooftop, we have noted, represent man's desire to advance socially and financially, while the basement symbolizes his inability to do so. The historic plays, on the other hand, all of which were written after 1958, employ an "open" or "epic" structure, plastic effects, and devices usually associated with Brecht, such as narrators like Valentín Haüy in the epilogue to *The Concert at Saint Ovide*. Although no illusion of reality is created, the emotional involvement of the spectator is preserved; for as we have seen, Buero considers that both critical reflection and emotive participation are essential. Whereas the first group of plays are psychological in emphasis, the historical ones are dialectical or ideological.

CHAPTER 6

The Search for Truth:
Idealism versus Realism

"None of us is without guilt."
—*El sueño de la razón* (*The Sleep of Reason*)[1]

THE tragedies in the preceding chapters depict the spiritual (or physical) blindness of the protagonists and their search for "light"—a search which is very explicit in the case of Amalia in *Dawn*, Enrique in *The Awaited Sign*, Silverio in *Today's a Holiday*, and Juan in *The Cards Face Down*, as well as Daniel in *The Double Case History of Dr. Valmy*. Mario's quest for understanding in *The Basement Window* and David's for vision or insight to triumph over his physical handicap are equally manifest. Other tragedies, however, show society, as a whole, to be blind—as does *The Concert at Saint Ovide*. In the historical plays and the fantasies to be analyzed below, the protagonists seek to bring the light of understanding to a nation or society obscured by social injustice, moral decadence, and war. These tragedies thus constitute a search for the comprehension which will permit society as well as the individual to surmount its limitations, although the protagonists achieve self-realization through their efforts on behalf of their fellowmen. These plays include *Un soñador par un pueblo* (*A Dreamer for a People*), 1958; *Las Meninas* (*The Ladies-in-Waiting*), 1960; *El sueño de la razón* (*The Sleep of Reason*), 1970, *Aventura en lo gris* (*Adventure in Grey*), 1963; and *Mito* (*Myth*), 1968.

The protagonist in these plays is usually a dreamer or visionary like Mario, who dreams of a perfect society in *The Basement Window*. More often than not, he is a rebellious dreamer like David, who struggles to put his dreams into action. Since these protagonists include an enlightened politician in *A Dreamer for a People*, artists in *The Ladies-in-Waiting* and *The Sleep*

107

of Reason, and a university professor in *Adventure in Grey,* these
tragedies constitute a statement about the role of the intellectual
in society. A recent statement by Buero on what he considers his
own role is significant in this respect. When asked, in a poll
of Spanish intellectuals and artists, whether he considers himself isolated from or integrated into the society he lives in, he
replies:

Integrated, because I as a person and my work represent nothing
without an effective response on the part of many of my fellowmen.
Integrated, for I consider that society is perfectible; perhaps I can
do my small part toward that goal. Integrated, also, because I am
not indifferent to its errors and injustices. They are, in part, mine
and I want to combat them in society and in myself. Integrated, and
yet, out of step. For this reason, at times, I need a certain distance,
a certain solitude, which unites me even more profoundly [to society]
through criticism, reflection, and rebellion.[2]

I   Un soñador para un pueblo (A Dreamer for a People)

Esquilache, the idealistic reformer of *A Dreamer for a People,*
who dreams of educating and civilizing Spanish society, is not
very different from David in *The Concert at Saint Ovide.* Like
the latter, he rebels against "the stubborn blindness of the
nation." His aims are expressed symbolically when he speaks of
bringing "a bit of light, of joy" to a people in "sad darkness."
A concrete symbol of the "light" or truth which he attempts
to bring is the lanterns which he orders installed in the streets
of Madrid.

*A Dreamer for a People: Free Version of an Historical Epi-
sode* is dedicated to the memory of Antonio Machado, "who
dreamed of a young Spain." The play, which deals with the
efforts of Charles III's liberal minister Esquilache to enlighten
a backward nation, has been termed by Torrente Ballester "one
of the few serious attempts to understand the history of Spain
since Lope de Vega."[3] The play concerns the minister of a monarch whose reign is undoubtedly one of the most polemical in
Spanish history. It depicts the unsuccessful attempt of the
ilustrados, or more enlightened thinkers, to transform Spain into
a modern nation. Buero explains that since these intellectuals
and their exceptional monarch have long suffered a "bad press,"

he has attempted to give them a sort of dramatic reparation. The play thus defends the "Enlightened Spain" which Esquilache, who as a historical figure may be of debated merit, symbolizes for dramatic purposes.[4] The dreams of the *ilustrados,* Buero adds, are especially relevant, for many things in Spain today resemble those against which they fought. Esquilache institutes various reforms designed to realize his dreams. He paves the streets of Madrid, installs five thousand lanterns in the streets, and combats the immorality at court—including bribery and favoritism— as well as the pilfering and killing in the streets by *embozados* or muffled figures. The play is based on the violent Madrid riot on Palm Sunday of 1766 which was provoked by Esquilache's edict banning the wearing of broad-brimmed slouch hats and long capes on the ground that they made it easy to escape arrest, an edict which he believes will reduce the number of crimes committed with impunity and which represents a step in the right direction.

However, as in *The Concert at Saint Ovide,* the dreamer is misunderstood and rejected by all. The attitude of the reactionaries toward Esquilache's reforms and toward the Enlightenment is seen in the following conversation with the Duke de Villasanta, which is illustrative of the problems of "the two Spains":

ESQUILACHE: Do you think that I'm an enemy of everything Spanish? I have learned to love this land. But it is not our fault if your lordships, you who consider yourselves genuine representatives of the Spanish soul, aren't capable of adding new glory to so many dead glories . . .

VILLASANTA: Dead?

ESQUILACHE: Believe me, my lord. There's nothing worse than being dead and not knowing it. Your lordships lament the fact that the principal ministers are foreigners, but the king brought us with him from Italy because the country needs us to elevate it. Nations must change if they don't want to die completely.

VILLASANTA: In what direction? In the direction of the "Enlightenment?" What your lordships call "the light of knowledge?" We call it heresy.[5]

The ideological issues of the play go back to Larra, Galdós, and, more recently, the Generation of 1898.

110 ANTONIO BUERO VALLEJO
Esquilache is opposed, however, not only by the reactionaries, but also by intelligent, liberal nobles who, although they realize that Spain needs reform, desire power above all else. The Marquis de la Ensenada, although he initiated many of the very reforms which Esquilache has carried out, organizes the uprising from jealousy because Esquilache has supplanted him in the king's favor. However, Ensenada is motivated not only by opportunism, but also by cynicism. The following dialogue concerning the edict on hats and capes contrasts Ensenada's and Esquilache's views of the *pueblo* or common people:
ENSENADA: .We've needed that measure for years and now is the time to enforce it with a firm hand.
ESQUILACHE: But it's not a question of a firm hand.
ENSENADA: Reform can't be handled in any other way. Remember our motto: "Everything for the people, but without the people." The people are always minors.
ESQUILACHE: I don't think you interpret those words correctly . . . "Without the people," not because they must be minors, but because they are still minors.
ENSENADA: You won't go far with those illusions. I lost mine twenty years ago. Have they given even one sign of understanding? Are they even grateful for what you do for them? You've elevated the country, you've given them education, welfare funds for widows and orphans, you've abolished hunger. You've shown them, in short, that life can be sweet. . . .And so, they hate you. (p. 23)
Here, as in *The Concert at Saint Ovide*, we see the loneliness of the dreamer. The blind incomprehension of those around him extends even to his own family. "I fear your quixotism," Esquilache's wife says to him. "Don't presume to be such an idealist." Just as David is misunderstood and rejected by everyone except Adriana, Esquilache is misunderstood by all except the king and Fernandita, a humble servant girl who, grateful for his efforts to elevate the people, becomes his friend and confidante. Esquilache's situation is quite similar to Dr. Stockmann's in Ibsen's play, *An Enemy of the People*. The doctor attempts to convince the people of his town that their famous Baths are contaminated and causing illness. However, for trying to enlighten society, he is misunderstood and branded "an enemy of the people." Reviled and ridiculed not only by the

reactionary officials, but by the liberals and "the ignorant majority," who fear their income will be lost, he is understood only by his daughter Petra.

Together with the reactionary forces exemplified by Villasanta, Ensenada succeeds in inciting the worst elements of the people. The rejection of the dreamer and of the "light" which he attempts to bring is symbolized by the mob's destruction of the lanterns which he has had constructed. The spiritual blindness of the nation is thus shown visually by Buero's skillful use of contrasting light and darkness. "It's getting dark now," Esquilache remarks to Fernandita the night before the uprising, "we're like children in the darkness. (*Suddenly a lantern is lit outside, somewhere nearby, and its light illuminates the couple in the window . . .*) Look. The darkness is over. Soon they'll light all the lanterns in Madrid. The dirtiest city in Europe will be the most beautiful, thanks to me. It is impossible for them not to thank me" (p. 64). Then, one by one other lanterns are lit in front of Esquilache's house until the stage is brightly illuminated. But shortly after Esquilache has commented upon their beauty, cloaked figures appear with rocks and break them. Then there is darkness. After Esquilache's house has been stoned and ransacked, and after he and Fernandita have taken refuge in the royal palace the next evening, Esquilache remarks: "Now it's night. . . . And very dark. . . . Madrid doesn't sparkle as it once did" (p. 81).

The idealist who clashes with reality is finally forced to abandon his reforms and go into exile. Nevertheless, this exile represents an interior triumph. The king, who Esquilache believes has abandoned him, comes on the night of the uprising to tell him that the decision is his: his exile, which the mob is demanding, or the danger of a bloody civil war. Esquilache sacrifices himself for the ultimate realization of his dreams. Esquilache's decision to go into exile obviously represents an internal victory. Esquilache serenely accepts his external defeat as the price he must pay for personal weaknesses, including ambition, years ago. He then asks Fernandita's pardon. Her words, however, are not of pardon, but of gratitude; for even though Esquilache has failed in his reforms, he has prevented an immensity of suffering.

Esquilache's last official act is to give to Ensenada, on whose

behalf he has spoken to the king, a letter which he supposes is
an appointment, but which turns out to be an order for Ensenada's exile. Esquilache now realizes for the first time that Ensenada was a secret instigator of the uprising. "The king," he states,
"has brought us face to face to compare us." It is not the reactionary Villasanta who is contrasted to the protagonist, but
Ensenada, the enlightened, intelligent, but cynical ex-minister
who began many of the reforms which Esquilache has carried
on but who no longer dreams, and who now considers Esquilache's hopes for the people illusions. Whereas Ensenada, the
cynic, has conspired to start a disastrous civil war, Esquilache
has prevented it.

Here, as in all Buero's theater, we see the insufficiency or
the limits of reason alone. It is important to note, in this regard,
that Esquilache himself is presented, as the title indicates, primarily as a dreamer, rather than an *ilustrado*. When Ensenada
says that he is intellectually superior to Esquilache, the latter
does not deny it. "Nevertheless," he answers, "I am greater
than you. The most insignificant man is greater than you if he
lives for something other than himself!" (pp. 99-100). Without
dreams it is impossible to remain free from corruption. The
rationalist who does not dream becomes a searcher for power,
for advantage.

Although Esquilache goes down to external defeat, there remains the hope that his dreams will one day become realities.
This hope is represented by Fernandita, who represents the
good qualities of the people. Pursued and seduced during the
uprising by Bernardo el Calesero, a leader of the mob, Fernandita has seemed unable to resist him although he represents all
the stupidity and brutality which she hates. "It is the cruel
blindness of life," Esquilache says to her. "But you can open
your eyes. [...] You must triumph through your own freedom....
I believe in you, Fernandita. The people aren't the devils you've
seen. The people are you! They're in you. [...] Perhaps their sad
darkness will never become light.... But it's up to you!" (p.
104). At the end, hope appears justified as Fernandita breaks her
relationship with Bernardo. Here, as in *The Basement Window*
where the investigators announce the achievement of a more
perfect society, Buero expresses his faith in human progress. After chronicling the errors of the people, he shows them capable

of overcoming the verdict of history and, through their own efforts, creating a more just society.

Although set in the eighteenth century, the relevance of the play to contemporary Spain is obvious. Esquilache symbolizes the application of intelligence to political power and the openness to external influence necessary to any epoch, under any circumstances. The performance of the play gave rise to violent polemics. The work was unjustly attacked both by those who consider the *ilustrados* excessively liberal and, like *An Enemy of the People*, by those who charged that the playwright was defending reactionaries. The play was likewise condemned, by some who perhaps did not wish to understand Buero's message, as an attack upon the people—despite the explicit faith he expresses in it. Such polemics, of course, are proof of the play's extraordinary impact.

II   Las Meninas (The Ladies-in-Waiting)

The epoch of Philip IV, another disastrous period in Spain's history, is dramatized in *The Ladies-in-Waiting: a Fantasy in Two Parts about Velázquez*. Doménech remarks that this play, which portrays Velázquez' attempts to express the economic and moral decadence of his epoch, reflects "the essence of the Generation of 1898: its critical spirit, its sense of historical responsibility, its love for and deeply-felt sorrow over Spain."[6]

Buero Vallejo presents the court painter as the historical conscience of his time, as a rebel who protests oppression, falsity, and hypocrisy. Buero states that Velázquez has always interested him as a man, misunderstood and worthy of revindication. Buero maintains that the biographical data available even though scanty, refute the charges of Velázquez' support of existing institutions, his vain pretensions to nobility, and his obsequious deference to authority. The data show us a man who was independent, critical, and entirely honest; who, like Quevedo and Gracián, kept his eyes open in a world blinded with error, superstition, and injustice.[7] The dramatist therefore considers the painter an appropriate figure for the exposition of certain problems of continuing importance in Spain. These problems, Buero suggests, are blindness to reality, social injustice, human misery—and the intellectual's responsibility in these areas. As Pedro, Velázquez' beggar friend, suggests in the play, perhaps the artist, who sees the beauty of the world, can best understand its sorrow. In Buero's play Velázquez is confronted by constant reminders of Spain's economic and moral decay. Money is lacking to pay the palace servants, and the common people are crushed by taxes to support the throne and the nobility, while Philip builds new parks. Dwarfs are exploited and derided in the palace under the guise of philanthropy—just as blindmen were ridiculed at the Fair of St. Ovide—and the king sires illegitimate children. But worst of all is the hypocrisy and pretense. In short, Spain is "a country of blindmen and lunatics."[8]

In such an atmosphere, Velázquez, the man of superior intellect, strives, like Esquilache, to reveal the truth. The nude Venus which he paints in defiance of the prohibitions of the Holy Office is symbolic of the truth he strives to bring: "Hunger grows, grief increases, the air becomes poisoned, and truth isn't tolerated. It must hide like my Venus because it is naked" (p. 123). The truth which Velázquez attempts to paint about the Spain of his time is evident in his sketch for his proposed painting, The Ladies-in-Waiting. Aesthetically, Velázquez' method of painting, his famous "abbreviated style" with its lack of detail, represents an innovation in his time—an attempt to paint the impression that objects leave upon the eye for a fleeting moment. This method represents for Velázquez a more faithful way of painting. It is by means of this method that Velázquez attempts to paint his vision of the truth about Spain. For Buero, Velázquez' painting is much more than an aesthetic phenomenon. It supposes a judgment on, or perhaps an idea of Spain. And this provides the inspiration for Buero's reconstruction of Velázquez's moral character, for his conception of Velázquez as a revolutionary painter and an essentially rebellious man.[9]

The truth about Spain which Velázquez attempts to reveal does not lie in her pomp or grandeur, but her "sadness" and "grief." The meaning of the sketch is explained by Pedro, the beggar who, with his near-blind eyes, is the only one who sees the truth that it represents:

A serene picture, but it enfolds all the sadness of Spain. Whoever sees these beings will understand how hopelessly condemned to grief they are. They are living ghosts of persons whose truth is death. Whoever looks at them tomorrow, will perceive it with fright. . . .

Yes, with fright, because the time will come, as it has come for me now, when one doesn't know if he himself is the ghost in sight of these figures . . . and he'll want to save himself with them, to embark on this immobile boat of a room, since they look at him, since he is already in the picture when they look at him . . . and perhaps, while he searches for his own face in the mirror in the rear he will be saved from death for a moment. (pp. 71-72)

However, it is not only the problem of Spain which Veláz-quez attempts to express in *The Ladies-in-Waiting*, but also the question about the ultimate meaning of "light." The artist explains that his painting is "a picture of poor mortals saved by the light. . . . I have come to suspect that the very form of God, if he has any, would be that of light. . . . It cures me of all the world's madness. Suddenly I see . . . and peace envelops me" (p. 72).

"The truth is a terrible burden; it's a sacrifice to stand alone." With these words Velázquez expresses the loneliness of the superior man in a world of lies and hypocrisy he cannot accept —the same loneliness experienced by Esquilache. This loneliness, as in Esquilache's case, extends even to his personal life, for his wife is utterly incapable of understanding either him or his paintings. Only Pedro, the near-blind beggar who served as Velázquez' model for *Aesop* years ago, is capable of understanding the painter's work. Pedro, together with the other beggar who was the model for *Menippus*, serves as narrator at times—like the blind calendar vendor in *A Dreamer for a People*. When Pedro returns, after years of leading rebellions against injustice and oppression in various parts of the country, Velázquez realizes that it is for him that he has painted all these years. He finds truth in the fugitive from the law who believes as he does. Pedro, who once wanted to be a painter himself, has spent six years in the galleys. "The sea is beautiful," he tells his friend, "but an oar is not a paintbrush. After being freed from the oar, there was little desire left to paint and I had to earn a living anyway I could" (p. 73). Both Pedro and Velázquez are rebels, but it is Pedro, who has put his rebellion into action, who is the true hero of the play. In Pedro Briones we have a romantic creation quite similar to that of Fernandita of the last play. Like Fernandita, Pedro symbolizes the people, who, despite perennial suppression, still struggle for freedom.

It is for sheltering Pedro as well as for his nude Venus and his sketch of *The Ladies-in-Waiting* that Velázquez is finally denounced. The trial scene, during which Velázquez combats the hypocritical morality of those envious of his position and defends his liberty as an artist and a man, is one of Buero's best —both for the dialectic as well as for the vivacious wit of Velázquez' replies. This trial is an invention of Buero, although the prohibition against nudity is, of course, historical. Denounced to the Holy Office, Velázquez first defends his Venus against "lewd minds" and his artistic freedom against arbitrary limitations. He must then defend his sketch of *The Ladies-in-Waiting* against the accusations of a rival who covets his position as court painter and who attacks the lack of solemnity and majesty in the royal subjects of *The Ladies-in-Waiting*—a lack of solemnity which makes the servants, dwarfs, and even the dog seem more important, for, in fact, Velázquez' painting serves as a leveler of society.

Accused finally of sheltering Pedro, a fugitive from the law, Velázquez protests against the misery and injustice ignored by the frivolous and idle courtiers of his time. It is after the marquis announces the capture, attempted escape, and death of Pedro that Velázquez makes his final decision between silence and protest—the choice which every intellectual must make "between truth or falsehood, between commitment or evasion, between rebellion or acquiescence."[10] He confesses to the king in unequivocal terms the "incurable rebelliousness" already implicit in his painting:

> On the one hand, falsehood. . . . A tempting falsehood which can only benefit me. On the other, truth. A dangerous truth which can't be of any help now. . . . If Pedro Briones were alive, he would repeat what he told me before I came here: lie if it is necessary. You must paint. But he is dead. Of what worth is our caution after that death? What can I give to be worthy of him if he has given his life? I couldn't lie even though I ought to. That poor dead man prevents me. . . . I offer you my sterile truth. . . . (*Forcefully!*) The truth, Sire, of my profound, my incurable rebelliousness! (pp. 122-23)

With this decision Velázquez thus wins an internal victory similar to Esquilache's. Surprisingly, the king reacts nobly, so that Velázquez is able to execute the painting.

The drama thus deals with the struggle of the intellectual who lives in a time of crisis—whether Velázquez' time or our own—to defend his liberty and, by using this liberty, to proclaim the truth. "Would you exile your conscience from the Palace?" the Infantita María Teresa asks her father on one occasion. Jean-Paul Borel states that of all Buero's characters, Velázquez is the one who most resembles his author; for Buero, like his Velázquez, is the conscience of his epoch.[11]

Buero's depiction of Velázquez as a rebel has given rise to strong disagreement on the part of critics. After suggesting that Buero perhaps found inspiration in Quevedo, who also was obsessed with the truth, Torrente defends the dramatist's interpretation, pointing out that if Velázquez painted the truth, it is legitimate to suppose that he defended it in his life.[12] To objections that it is unsound to imagine Velázquez in rebellion against the state and the king—in view of the aristocratic pretensions attributed to the historical Velázquez—and that Buero uses the painter as a pretext to voice his own political and social ideology, other critics have replied that the mere fact that as court painter Velázquez enjoyed the king's protection does not mean that we have to accept a "courtly Velázquez" and that in reality there are very few biographical data available.[13] Everything Velázquez has to say to us today is in his painting. Obviously Buero's rebellious protagonist is closer to the problematics, sensibilities, and hopes of our own time than the aristocratic courtier of Ortega y Gasset.[14]

III   El sueño de la razón (The Sleep of Reason)

Buero continues his dramatic inquiry into Spain's tragic destiny with *The Sleep of Reason*, which portrays another famous painter as the social conscience of his epoch. The play deals with the disastrous period following the War of Independence against the French, whose horrors Goya suggests in his enigmatic *Black Paintings*. Doménech points out that this epoch of civil discord under Fernando VII resembles the period during and immediately following the Spanish Civil War of the present century and that the play, therefore, is rigorously contemporary.[15] The tragedy takes place in December, 1823, after the overthrow of the liberal movement which lasted three years. It is the time of the restoration of absolutism and the accompanying terror, torture, and executions, which caused the emigration of many liberals.

Goya has resisted returning to the palace or rendering homage to Fernando despite the pleas of his mistress Leocadia de Weiss and despite insults by the mobs. A rebel, like Buero's Velázquez, he refuses to humiliate himself by asking Fernando's pardon even though he knows that his letter containing statements offensive to the king has been intercepted. Half hidden in his villa on the Manzanares, Goya paints and hopes to be forgotten. The king, however, in the royal palace—on the opposite bank of the river—works out an intricate plan to ensnare and entrap him. Nevertheless, Goya refuses to leave the country: "Accusations, persecutions . . . Spain. It is not easy to paint. But I shall paint!"[16] "I must paint here!" (p. 34).

Buero depicts the artist in his "hours of greatest lucidity and deepest darkness."[17] Like Velázquez, he is abandoned and alone —except for his mistress and his friends, Father José Duaso y Latre and Dr. Eugenio Arrieta. Goya's loneliness and isolation are heightened by his deafness—the result of a serious illness some thirty years before. The audience is made to share his handicap; for whenever Goya is on stage, the scenes are silent except for the words of the artist himself. The characters speak without articulating any sound at all, using sign language when they address the artist.

However, Goya's obsessions and hallucinations, the nightmares and horrors he experiences, are revealed through sound effects: meows, owl-hoots, and voices, often of figures from his own paintings. The words of Leocadia, who is thirty-five years younger than he, and of their young daughter Mariquita, particularly, permit us to enter Goya's inner world of doubts and insecurity caused by his declining virility. The voice of Mariquita, his absent daughter, urges him to challenge Leocadia, to present her with the proof of her supposed infidelity with an army sergeant. At the same time, the voices of the jesting women in his *Two Women and a Man* incite him to the solitary senile pleasures which his daughter urges him to forget.[18] The words Goya imagines said by the characters around him, like the other auditory hallucinations he experiences, demonstrate a capacity to apprehend reality which more than compensates for the deafness which symbolizes his isolation and estrangement—the same capacity which Pilar in *Today's a Holiday* possesses to a much lesser degree. The dispute Goya imagines between Leocadia and his daughter-in-law Gumersinda, for example, over the eventual disposition of his material possessions becomes a type of truth as their acrid words turn into cackling and braying—barnyard sounds which he perceives with both terror and amusement.

The playwright leads the audience to identify with his protagonist not only through sharing his deafness and "hearing" his thoughts, but, furthermore, through seeing the world through his eyes. To the vocalization of Goya's interior world, Buero adds its visualization—slides of the *Black Paintings* flashed on stage at appropriate times. The deaf man in *Two Monks* suggests Goya's own isolation. In *Judith and Holofernes,* the Israelite heroine cuts off the general's head after winning his affection, thus expressing the artist's fear of rejection.

Auditory and visual effects occur in most of Buero's theater. We have noted the farcical concert of blind men with their brightly colored robes and conical hats in *The Concert at Saint Ovide. The Ladies-in-Waiting* ends as the characters assume the positions of the persons in Velázquez' painting. However, Buero's sustained use of such effects in *The Sleep of Reason* is unprecedented in his previous plays. Juan Emilio Aragonés calls the work the first spectacle of "total theater" by a Spanish author.[19] Fernández-Santos points out that the play contains elements of each of the three major forms of contemporary theater—participation, distancing, and the absurd—all of which find their unity in the presentation of the sort of terror we see in the *Black Paintings* and in certain satiric-macabre scene such as the dispute between Leocadia and Gumersinda.[20]

Plunged into a world of silence from which it is difficult to communicate, Goya expresses both his own personal tragedy and that of Spain in the strange symbolic language of his *Black Paintings.* "What if those grotesques that he paints on the walls were masterpieces?" reasons Dr. Arrieta, "and what if his madness was his real strength?" (p. 84). Goya's fantastic murals, Buero believes, were the work of a mind basically sane but very near mental and emotional unbalance.[21]

"The sleep of reason produces monsters," states the inscrip-

tion to Goya's "Caprice 34." "Perhaps not always," decides Arrieta, "if reason is not completely dormant." Goya himself explains in his engraving: "Fantasy without reason produces mon-
strosities; but together they beget true art and may give rise
to wonderful things." Goya's paintings may thus be considered
the product of a reasoned fantasy. When reason sleeps, Royalist
thugs like Fernando VII appear whose madness is suggested by
the animal-like sounds Goya hears and by the monsters he depicts. When reason sleeps, Buero states in a commentary,[22]
a country should expect the worst, as should a great man. Nevertheless, his fear may result in his producing masterpieces of
satire. Goya's near, but not total, madness becomes a means of
apprehending reality more rigorously than it can be understood
through normality. We have seen that the insane father in *The
Basement Window* has profoundly lucid intuitions to which
the other characters cannot rise.

The artist himself suggests the meaning of his paintings, in
which he, like Velázquez in *The Ladies-in-Waiting*, attempts
to depict the truth about the Spain of his time: "The king,"
explains Goya, "is a monster and his advisors, jackals that he
incites not only to kill, but to steal. And they are sheltered, this
much is certain, by the law and the blessings of our prelates!
Despoil a liberal of his property? He had better not complain
or he would merit the gallows! We are not Spaniards but devils;
and they are angels fighting against hell. . . . But I get even. I
paint them with the faces of witches and goats at the witches'
Sabbaths which they call popular festivals" (p. 45).

Goya symbolizes the irrational and absurd evil he sees around
him as monsters—half-human, half-animal—terrifying creatures
that inhabit the mind during the sleep of reason. Goya's sur-
realism like Velázquez' "abbreviated style" is the method by
which the artist attempts to paint his vision of the reality of
Spain. For Goya, as for Velázquez, this reality lies in her death:

Lines of prisoners, insults of the rabble, perhaps dead men in
the gutters. [. . .] Men are beasts. And something else that I can't express. . . . Something else that I notice since I lost my hearing. Because
I entered another world . . . the other world. [. . .] Yes . . . People
laugh, make gestures, and speak to me. . . . I see them as dead beings.
And I wonder if I'm not the one who is dead, an observer of insects
crawling in the grave. I loved life. Lunches in the meadow, games,

songs, and maidens. . . . Then came my deafness and I understood
that life is death. A diminutive duchess laughs and sways in my
silence. She is a robot. [. . .] In the war I've seen people scream and
weep in the face of blood and mutilations. It was the same. Robots.
The bombs exploded and I could only imagine a ringing laughter.
(pp. 76-77)

John Kronik points out that Goya's criticism of a reality which
does not correspond to his ideals is the result not of hate, but
love—as is true also, in the case of Larra, Unamuno, and Buero
himself.[23]

Goya explains to his friends Arrieta and Duaso the meaning
of these enigmatic murals.[24] They reflect the painter's constant
conflict between fear and faith, doubt and hope—in regards
both to his country and himself as part of it. In *Fighting with
Clubs*, two men, who are clubbing each other with fratricidal
rage, gradually sink into the mire. Goya explains that he has
painted this barbarism because he has witnessed it, referring
to the War for Independence, with its brutality and atrocities
on both sides. "None of us," he realizes, "is without guilt." "Many
centuries ago," Goya reasons, "someone took by force what
wasn't his. With blows as from hammers. [. . .] And so we continue. Hammer in hand." Other paintings suggest the postwar
period. Saturn, symbol of cruelty and destruction, devours his son.
Members of the Holy Office conspire together, representatives of
the old inquisitorial and clerical Spain. In *The Return from
San Isidro*, we see the superstitions and prejudices that keep a
country which is not guided by reason paralyzed with fear and
unable to move forward. In *The Witches' Sabbath*, a mob of
bestial witches and warlocks listen, in darkness, to the preach-
ments of a cassocked ram, Satan. These figures, created by the
black mist swirling in Goya's mind, represent the invisible
forces of evil and destruction which possess Spain—in the artist's
epoch and in our own.

Even the *Black Paintings*, however, are not devoid of hope.
In the mythic *Asmodea*, a winged woman carries a man—who
is still terrified by the war, blood, and hate below—to a citadel
in the mountains, to the home of the flying men. Goya transforms
Asmodeo (the demon of lust from *The Book of Tobit*) into a
beautiful woman who, Goya dreams, will carry him away from
his miseries. Vaguely associated with his beloved Mariquita,

she represents Goya's hope for salvation and, moreover, his hopes for Spain. Goya tells Arrieta that he has actually seen these strange beings with their mechanical wings flying in the hills behind his villa. Not angels, but men, they are man's older brothers who perhaps have lived in the hills for centuries. Goya's greatest desire, he confesses, is for them to come down and do away with Fernando VII and all the cruelties on earth. Perhaps, he hopes, they will descend in a resplendent army and knock at all the doors in Madrid with blows so loud that Goya himself will hear them.[25] Blows as from tremendous hammers. Even the dreamer, however, is not totally convinced as to the reality of his visions. Goya struggles constantly between hope and doubt, between the "voices" and visions of the angelic Asmodea and of the monstrous demons pictured in the rest of the *Black Paintings*.

Goya's hopes for the flying men are seen once again at the end of the scene where Buero uses psychedelic lighting and sound effects to re-create the famous *caprice* whose inscription he uses as the play's title. As the artist sleeps, loud knocks are heard at the door, strange lights flood the room, and two masked figures appear: a man with enormous bat's wings and a woman with a cat's head and enormous teats. To the sounds of cowbells and laughter there then come in two pigs, with enormous hammers and rusty cowbells. Joined by a black-hooded figure with a skull-face and horns, they dance around Goya chanting grotesquely. When he attempts to escape, he is attacked, thrown to the floor, threatened by the uplifted hammers of the pigs, and finally condemned as a "Jew, freemason, liberal, Jacobin, an insolent and impertinent backslider, a painter, masturbator, and maker of images." The absurd ceremony, accompanied by nonsensical cries of "Long live the absolutely absolute king," etc., continues as Leocadia appears dressed as Judith. When she lifts her knife above Goya's head to execute him, the strange lights vanish and the paintings *Saturn, The Witches' Sabbath,* and *Judith and Holofernes* shine in the background. The entire scene has the same goyesque, esperpentesque quality as that of Gumersinda and Leocadia's cackling and braying and that of the orchestra in *The Concert at Saint Ovide*. It ends as loud knocking is heard on the door. To the noise of gigantic wing beats resounding in the air, Goya awakens from the sleep into which he has again fallen. An extraordinary hope shines in his eyes as he announces that the flying men are knocking at all the doors in Madrid.

The knocks, it turns out, announce the arrival not of flying men, but of five soldiers, with sabers and perverse, leering faces. They have been sent by the king to humiliate Goya. Not daring to execute so famous an artist, the king seeks to force him to beg for pardon. That the soldiers' attack has been prefigured by Goya's dream, an *esperpento* or caricature of what now occurs, is further evidence that Goya's visions and "voices" constitute, in fact, a revelation of truth. The soldiers throw the artist to the floor, beat him with their sabers, put on him the inquisitorial *sanbenito* and conical hat, and place in his hands a black wooden cross—thus transforming him into one of the penitents he used to paint. Goya is finally encircled by three soldiers who silently threaten him with their hammers and chant, wordlessly, insulting verses heard in the dream. The climax is Leocadia's rape by the sergeant as we hear deafening heartbeats, donkey-brays, chicken-cackles, and terrifying shrieks. This pandemonium is gradually replaced by laughter and by voices, which enunciate appropriate inscriptions selected from the *Disasters of War* and the *Caprices*: "For this you were born." "Don't cry, foolish girl." "They are wild beasts." These voices continue intermittently accompanied by Goya's own voice: "Truth is dead." "Divine reason, don't spare any of them."[26]

Goya's political defeat is thus paralleled by his personal tragedy. After the soldiers leave, Goya accuses his mistress of having brought them so that she might enjoy herself. Then we hear the words that Goya imagines Leocadia speaks, words which evince all the insight of his hallucinations. She is, she confesses, guilty, but Goya is too. She has loved him without really understanding him. Proof of her love is her remaining with him to care for him. She was forced to endure the sergeant's brutality because they were at his mercy, but perhaps was guilty of desiring him.

In the end, the artist goes down to outward defeat, as do Buero's other rebellious dreamers. There is no solution left for the artist but to accept Duaso's help in securing permission to leave for France. Goya is but an old man on the verge of the grave in a country which is ready for death and whose reason

sleeps. His inner victory is the paintings he leaves on the walls
of the villa; and the sight of them comforts him at his departure.
When he leaves, the voices repeat over and over, until the end
of the play, the title of one of his *Caprices*: "If morning comes,
we will go!"—indicative of his hope for the dawn that will, as
in his engraving, drive away the witches. He is not, however,
without doubts: "Will the flying men come? And if they come,
won't they beat us like dogs?" The tragedy thus ends ambivalently as the deafening din of the voices invades the room. In
The Sleep of Reason, as in the preceding two plays, Buero dram-
atizes certain negative moments in Spain's history to illustrate
problems whose essence and reality are still present today and
to point out the need for tolerance and intelligence. In these
plays, no less than in *Story of a Stairway, Today's a Holiday,* and
The Cards Face Down, we see the tragedy of present-day Spain.

IV   Aventura en lo gris (Adventure in Gray)

The strong antiwar sentiment suggested by Esquilache's
voluntary exile to avoid civil war, and certain of Goya's *Black
Paintings,* as well as by Penelope's condemnation of Ulysses'
abandonment of his home to fight and the plight of the family
in *The Basement Window* after the Spanish Civil War becomes
paramount in *Adventure in Gray*.

Like Esquilache, Velázquez, and Goya, Silvano, the protagonist of *Adventure in Grey,* longs to bring to society the light of
understanding. In the sordid gray reality of Surelia, an imaginary
country just defeated and overrun by enemy soldiers with
machine guns, he strives to impart his dream of peace: "There
is a dream that I have repeatedly. . . . I find myself in a vast
green field abundant with tranquil water. Beautiful, smiling
beings pass by me. Proud matrons, girls and boys brimming
with majesty, old men with silver hair and children with amber
locks. They are all like angels without wings."[27]

The tragedy, two acts separated by a fantastic dream, takes
place one night at a somber gray and brown shelter where
several refugees await a train to evacuate them. One of these
refugees is Silvano, a history professor who has been dismissed
and exiled as the result of his doubts as to the wisdom of continuing the war—when the government is already secretly pre-

paring to surrender—and of his statements that neither side was completely blameless. Silvano is not entirely sure that his position was correct. A man of doubt, not certainty, he has asked himself if he did right. People often need lies, he realizes, to go on. Historians of the future, he decides, will be his judge. Other refugees include Alejandro, the leader of the defeated guerrillas and the man responsible for Silvano's exile; Ana, Alejandro's disenchanted mistress; Carlos, a member of his party; Isabel, a poor peasant girl whom Carlos is accompanying; Isabel's baby, the fruit of a brutal attack by an enemy soldier; a peasant who refuses to share his bread with the others; and Georgina, a rich woman whose money is safely invested abroad. Before all retire for the night, Silvano speaks of the importance which he attaches to dreams:

SILVANO: To learn to dream would be to learn to live. We all dream of the most secret appetites and at night we let loose the beast within us. But if we would only learn.

[..]

Do we have bad dreams because we behave badly during the day or do we act basely in life because we don't know how to have good dreams? It's not easy to answer, is it?

[..]

Perhaps both things are true. But then, also, one must learn to dream. . . . Suppose people who know each other well began to have the same dream?

ANA: The same dream?

SILVANO: It's not impossible. If our minds would become more flexible so they could transmit or receive thoughts . . .

ALEJANDRO: (*Scornfully.*) Telepathy.

SILVANO: Something like that. Dreams would become a prolongation of life, but more open; we would dream the same dream and the very clash of our selfish desires would prevent their fulfillment. We would see ourselves as we are inside and, perhaps, when we awakened we could not go on pretending. We would have to improve. . . . For it is in our dreams that we find our truest essence. (pp. 44-45)

It will be useless, Silvano believes, for men to serve in commissions and in governments, unless they are led by dreams which have become reconciled.

"Poor dreamer," Alejandro, the man of action, replies to
Silvano's dreams of peace. "Dreaming," he believes, "is for
women. . . . or contemplatives." Nevertheless, Silvano hopes to
prove during the contest he senses has begun that he is more
useful to his country than Alejandro, who has left behind him
a trail of dead comrades and violated women, and who is,
moreover, now fleeing even though he has promised to remain
to lead the guerrillas.

That night all except Alejandro have a common prophetic
dream, although only Silvano and Ana are permitted to understand that the mystery of which the former spoke has actually
occurred. As the setting is transformed into an indistinct room
illuminated by a cold white light through whose windows sub-
marine life is seen, and the music of Debussy's "Sirènes" is
heard, the characters act out their subconscious desires. Ana,
exploited and destroyed by Alejandro, reveals her love for
Silvano, urging him to descend from his height while he, seated
on a high mount dreaming, encourages her to come up to him.
The avaricious farmer appears as a rich man who caresses his
golden bread. Bread, which should be a promise of peace,
abundance, and love, as Silvano notes, becomes a ferment of
hatred. As mocking faces of enemy soldiers appear at the windows, Isabel relives her violation. Finally, Carlos, her protector,
reveals his own desire for her and when she refuses him, urged
by Georgina who wants him for herself, he puts his hands to
her neck as if to strangle her. It is this dream which leads Pérez
Minik to call the play the most daring, in its formal structure,
of all Buero's works up to 1961.[28]

With the return to reality at dawn, Isabel is, in fact, found
dead. However, Silvano proves that she was murdered not by
Carlos, but by Alejandro, after he was unable to seduce her.
Alejandro thus exposes himself as an ambitious and unscrupulous egoist "accustomed to taking money, luxury, women as he
goes. [. . .] A man . . . of action, who never dreams . . . and who
acts while others sleep" (p. 91). "I was mad," exclaims Ana,
"to share your life and believe the reasons you used to justify
it. [. . .] You derided everything and stained it . . . in the name of
efficiency" (p. 92). The contrast between Silvano, the intellectual
dreamer or idealist, and Alejandro, the practical man of action,
is similar to the opposition of Ulysses and Anfino, and, especially,

Vicente and Mario. Just as Vicente sacrifices Beltrán in his search for success at any cost and victimizes his secretary Encarna, so Alejandro has betrayed his men and exploited Ana. As Mario dreams of a perfect world while he contemplates through the window the struggle in the world outside, so Silvano, seated on high, in his dream, envisions a world of peace. Ana, moreover, like Encarna, represents the victim of oppression.

Alejandro loses his contest with Silvano; for, without dreams, the man of action becomes corrupt—as we have already seen in the case of Ensenada, in *A Dreamer for a People,* who betrays his people out of egoism. Silvano wins the contest because he is able to put his dreams into action. When it becomes apparent that no train will arrive and the refugees flee at the approach of the enemy, Silvano decides to stay behind in order to persuade the enemy soldiers to care for Isabel's baby—an innocent being in whom the blood of two enemy peoples may meet in a definitive embrace, a child who may become tomorrow a man free from hatred. One theme of the play, Buero states, is "that of righteous action, personified in a seemingly spineless dreamer who, without pretension, is capable of the most dauntless heroism."[29] Ana, even knowing that it will cost her her life, chooses to remain behind with him. Both thus win an internal victory; they have learned, in Silvano's words, "what it means to triumph" and "what it means to triumph over oneself."

Their last moments are ones of happiness, for they have been able to illuminate the grayness of their lives with an "adventure of light." As the soldiers raise their guns, they face death without fear, bathed in the rays of the morning sun which enters the windows of the squalid shelter, dissipating the darkness of human egoism.

When the curtain falls, the sordid gray of reality has not been changed; men have not learned to "dream in unison"; and the enemy soldiers are still "exterminators with machine guns," not the smiling angels of whom he dreams. To Silvano's question, "Who are you," the soldiers who appear at the windows during his dream reply, "your angels without wings." At the end of the play, Silvano's dreams of peace have not been realized—dreams echoed in a moving sonnet of Buero published in *Cuadernos de Agora*:

With crowns of victory and peace,
and purged of all extremes, we'll see
how man with man is reconciled with ease.[30]

Nevertheless, one of the soldiers has agreed to evacuate the
baby so that they may find milk. Whereas Pilar's baby in *Today's
a Holiday*—also the result of a violation by an enemy soldier—
and the baby in *The Basement Window* die, Isabel's baby, who
represents hope for the future, is saved. Universal in its message,
the play lends itself to various interpretations.[31] In its author's
words, it represents "merely another outcry [. . .] on behalf of
man and his suffering humanity, always in danger and so often
trampled upon."[32]

V Mito: libro para una ópera (Myth: Libretto for an Opera)

Like the pacifistic professor in *Adventure in Gray*, the incarnation of kindness and generosity, many of Buero's protagonists
are dreamers or visionaries who bear the indelible stamp of
Don Quijote. Upon none, however, is the Cervantine influence so
strong as upon Eloy, the old actor in *Myth* who once played the
role of Don Quijote himself and who is considered mad by his
fellow players because he believes in flying saucers and Martians. *Myth* is Buero's only theatrical work in verse.

He explains the title of his work by saying that one of the
universal human and literary myths of all times is that of Don
Quijote. One of the great myths of our own period is that of
flying saucers (of which the myth of Asmodea and the flying
men in *The Sleep of Reason* is an interesting precursor). Buero
states that the title of his present work is in the singular because
both myths are related and, in fact, interwoven.[33]

Eloy of *Myth* represents the moral idealist. While bombs explode and curfews are imposed by the government—curfews
said to be part of air raid drills, but believed by the workers
to be screens for the purpose of concealing their strikes—Eloy,
like Silvano of *Adventure in Gray*, dreams of peace. Inspired—
or deranged—not by novels of chivalry, but of science fiction, he
believes that the bombs signify the imminent landing of visitors
from Mars. These visitors will save man from the folly of a war
which would annihilate him and will usher in a new era of
peace. Just as Don Quijote casts himself in the role of a knight-

errant charged with restoring the Age of Gold, Eloy believes himself the instrument chosen to announce the visitors, whose arrival the government wants to conceal. Of all Buero's protagonists, Eloy most closely resembles Silvano. However, Eloy's belief in the visitors' arrival is similar to Goya's faith in the descent of flying men who will put an end to all the cruelties on earth. As we shall see, *Myth* and *The Sleep of Reason* present interesting similarities.

His mission, Eloy believes, has been imparted to him by a detector placed by Martians in the saucer-like barber's basin which Don Quijote took for the helmet of Mambrino. Eloy has caressed and cherished this basin ever since that night he played the hero's role. Eloy also believes that the presence of Martians among men on earth has been revealed. One of these Martians is Marta, a humble servant girl at the theater. The voices of the Martians which are heard by Eloy obviously parallel those Goya hears, especially the encouraging one of Asmodea-Mariquita.

Considered mad by all, Eloy discloses the mystery of the helmet only to Simón, who parallels the role of Don Quijote's faithful squire, and to whom Eloy has promised the position of mayor of the city when the Martians arrive. Struck by Eloy in a certain place, the helmet emits a cataract of crystalline notes which form a strange melody and which continue to sound as Simón listens. It is the ineffable music of the helmet through which the Martians speak to Eloy and whose effluence, he believes, is invading the world in order to save it. The fact that this music is actually heard by Simón and the audience does not necessarily mean that it cannot be imaginary. If it were *not* perceived physically, it would obviously be an illusion of Eloy, whom the other characters consider a madman. Such ambivalence is common in the theater of Buero, who attempts to make the spectator think.

Eloy's faith seems confirmed with the arrival of visitors in what is actually a dream. As he sits alone on the stage steps and his eyes gradually close, the music imitates the melody emitted by the helmet; a cold white undulating light illuminates the stage; and six figures in sparkling metallic suits and green masks appear to announce that they have come, not as gods but as brothers, to bring a new era of peace.

Just as Don Quijote is told that he is to announce to the world

what lies buried in the cave of Montesinos, Eloy is ordered to
announce the arrival of the Martians. Even as Montesinos tells
Don Quijote that it is by his aid and favor that he and Belerma,
along with the others, may be disenchanted—for great deeds are
reserved for great men—so the visitors announce to Eloy that
he is the one chosen by them to prepare men for the coming
of the new reign of peace. Eloy must be prepared, however,
for great trials and suffering because the Martians have not come
to conquer militarily. If direct intervention is not necessary,
they will remain hidden and Eloy will face the bitter test of
hopelessness. To accompany him in his loneliness, however,
Mars gives him the love of Marta. Only Eloy is worthy of her
love. Like Dulcinea, who appears to Don Quijote in the cave,
Marta comes to Eloy and offers him her love and urges him
to maintain his faith. Soon, she tells him, the music of Mars
will fill his world with peace. Like Dulcinea and like Melania,
the lovely blind lady David dreams of and talks to in *The Concert
at Saint Ovide*, she represents the ideal.

Real or imagined, Eloy's vision is efficacious. Just as Silvano's
dream of peace motivates him to save an innocent child, Eloy's
leads him to shelter Ismael, the old union leader who has devoted
his life to the oppressed and who is now pursued by the police
in an effort to terminate a strike. Eloy's idealism is put to the
test when he hides Ismael, who, like the others, dismisses his
visions of the new era of justice as merely "beautiful dreams."
Even if the Martians were not coming, the idealist replies, he
would protect him because "if anyone suffers injustice/ it is
our duty to help him."[34]

Those around Eloy—like those around Don Quijote and those
around Buero's many characters in whom Don Quijote reappears
—are blind to the spiritual reality represented by his visions.
The priests and Sansón Carrasco, afraid to open their eyes lest
the security of their comfortable world be challenged, reject
Don Quijote's contention that there are giants to be slain or
enchanters who enslave men's minds. Goya's countrymen consider his *Black Paintings* madness; and Silvano's companions
dismiss his dreams of angels without wings as insanity. So the
electrician who works on stage smugly assures Eloy that his
visions of impending judgment by the Martians—a time when
man will be forced to see himself as he really is—are illusions,

as are, also, his dreams of ultimate salvation. To Eloy's belief that he is not alone but accompanied by millions of celestial beings, the electrician, unable to comprehend any reality higher than that of his science, replies that there are no Martians, only the inexhaustible field of electricity; no mysteries, only hallucinations. "Electrician," Eloy tells him, "return to your control room./ Don't pontificate about what you know nothing." "He who doesn't know that he is ignorant is not a wise man," he adds, "he is merely a sacristan of magnetism" (pp. 57-58). The superior vision implied by Eloy's name is suggestive of the lucid intentions of the insane father in *The Basement Window* who, as we have seen, Doménech speculates may be a God-figure.[35]

The electrician, who actually feels a bit of affection toward Eloy, simply rejects the dreamer's faith. However, other members of the theatrical company—morally corrupt like the duke and duchess in *Don Quijote,* and more than a bit envious of Eloy—ridicule his visions. For the actors' amusement, moreover, Eloy is made the object of a joke far crueler than Don Quijote's ride on Clavileño. To the accompaniment of blinding lights, there suddenly appear two strange figures who announce that their flying squadrons from Jupiter have already devastated Mars and are even now overrunning Earth and enslaving, without pity, its inhabitants—weaklings whom they despise.

Eloy, the only one of the startled actors who shows no fear, is told that he must prove his valor by taking a trip in their spacecraft. As the two actors who are the authors of the joke make explanations to the other members of the cast—all of whom seem paralyzed with fright—Eloy and Simón are lifted blindfolded into the air on two chairs. Bright lights from missiles said to be destroying Martian cities are simulated by lanterns moved in front of their faces; and the bombing and disintegration of Mars' satellites are represented by the explosions outside the theater. The agony of the survivors is feigned by the neighing, hooting, howling, and screeching of the actors, who encircle the travelers with orgiastic dances and beastly laughter in an esperpentesque scene reminiscent of the re-creation of Goya's caprice. It is in the midst of this delirium that Eloy's voice rises, pure and serene, under the starry night depicted on the rear curtain, to sing his song of faith to a distant galaxy of peace. Despite his doubt and seeming defeat, he expresses to the invaders his conviction that, despite the tragedy of Mars, their insane efforts to spread destruction will fail:

> I sing of peace, of honor, and intelligence
> and send my verses to a distant galaxy.
> She keeps a vigil with her clear and watchful eyes
> and piously awaits the death that will be yours
> before she sows the universe with seeds of grace.
> [..]
> Tremble in the wake of her untenable light,
> O victors, for she will have her certain triumph.
> Now, sad-eyed butchers, you may kill me if you wish.
> I send my verses to some far-off galaxy! (p. 81)[36]

Only after the visitors are unmasked does Eloy's faith turn into momentary disillusion. As flying saucers swiftly cross in front of the rear curtain and then fade into tiny spots of light which disappear, Eloy admits that perhaps he is a madman unable to distinguish between reality and dreams, and that perhaps the Martians despise earthlings and will permit their destruction in the apocalypse they are preparing—if, indeed, Martians exist at all. Those who dream of peace may be fools; and their faith, insanity. However, if Eloy is mad, the world is no less so. For the frightful war simulated by the jokers is not in Heaven but on Earth. This very Cervantine conflict of dreams and reality is a major characteristic of Buero's theater. Just as the flying men who Goya believes are knocking on all the doors in Madrid turn out to be Fernando VII's soldiers sent to humiliate him, and the angel-like beings Silvano dreams of become enemy soldiers who kill him, so the men Eloy believes to be Martians turn out to be his own colleagues who are mocking him.

When the hero begins his second song, a lengthy catalogue of the ills of our time accompanied by horrifying visual effects in the background, the play becomes, among other things, an ironic indictment of modern civilization. "Our times," Eloy declares, "are, without a doubt, sweet and beautiful," as images of atomic mushrooms explode in the darkness and then give way to visions of extermination: heaps of dead cattle, insects, and men—the latter with crudely-sewn faces lacking eyes, noses, or ears. Due to "improvements" in science, weapons have become thermonuclear; and H-bombs will perhaps make the future impossible, he states. Therefore, Eloy will limit his remarks to the present. As burning books, gesticulating faces, shootings, hangings, and murders by garrote, guillotine, and electric chair are depicted in the background, Eloy sings his denunciation. Man prepares for war and believes he will have peace. He burns books and believes he is serving truth and goodness. To suppress dissidents, he calls them raving dogs. Man loves his children yet teaches them war, Eloy declares, as there appears on the back curtain a star which gradually becomes the huge image of a smiling child. On television, man demonstrates that spies are noble when they murder, and shows his children how their parents kill babies with napalm. He fills the air his children breathe with invisible poison and explodes bombs that spread imperceptible radiation which endangers future generations. And all the while he pretends that neither threat exists because he cannot see them. Mindful of the visitors' warning that he would be the butt of ridicule and jokes, Eloy, however, never loses his hope—even in the midst of despair and even ·when those who lack the sanity to stop death and destruction on earth mock him for envisioning help from another, better planet.

In the end, Eloy's hope is put to the supreme test, as he is warned it will be by the visitors whose voices he hears in a second dream, warning him that the great trial is approaching. Police arrive at the theater searching for Ismael, the activist and fugitive whom they have accused of burning a certain palace, in order to find a pretext to kill him and discredit the strikers he leads. In an effort to permit Ismael to escape, Eloy disguises himself and his friend and diverts the police who then chase and shoot him. When Ismael emerges from hiding and tries to surrender, it is too late. Eloy has been mortally wounded.

Eloy and Ismael present the contrast between the idealist dreamer and the man of action seen in many of Buero's plays. Like Alejandro in *Adventure in Gray,* Ismael tells the idealist, "You'll only be a dreamer/ if you don't forget your scruples/ and make up your mind to act." He plans to let an innocent man less useful to the cause die in his place if necessary. In the end, however, he has a change of heart, for he gives himself up to try to save Eloy.

Eloy, like Silvano, has given evidence of his faith by putting

his ideals into action. "To act," he replies to Ismael, "is to hide
you." Moreover, he believes that his action will not be useless.
When Ismael states that all their efforts have been futile and
that both are but fools, Eloy replies that their deeds are seeds
which will bear fruit. Quixotism, Buero believes, may be efficacious and lead to sane and dynamic social action. In a commentary, Buero explains his reasons for writing the work.[37] The
ideals of Don Quijote, he believes, have particular relevance for
contemporary times. Cervantes' hero created his faith in chivalry
in a grotesque and decadent society not unlike our own. It is
today's insane world, Buero believes, which leads quixotic individuals such as Eloy to their belief in flying saucers and "knights"
from Mars or Venus who will save man. He points out that the
faith of Don Quijote and belief in flying saucers indicate the
persistence in our own tortured and depraved world of certain
problems and questions common, also, to Cervantes' era. Buero
insists that the role of myth can always be positive, inspiring
man to useful action. But even if Don Quijote's faith is a com-
forting illusion or escape from reality, and if belief in flying
saucers is the same, both phenomena present certain symptoms of
a tragic world and demonstrate the need for change. Buero, however, makes clear that he considers both types of idealism as
tragedies open to further possibilities.

The play concludes enigmatically as the helmet, which has
fallen to the ground at Eloy's death, suddenly emits the strange
melody which the dreamer used to hear. Various members of
the cast who pass by pause to gaze at the fallen helmet, surprised—either by its music or simply by its unexpected presence.
When the curtain falls, the notes emitted by the helmet, which
have become a cascading melody, blend with the music from
the performance of Don Quijote, which the company is just
beginning.

"Bueroism" has been spoken of as a "search for love, faith,
justice, and, in short, peace. Or if one prefers, for truth," and
as a way of "understanding the problems of our time [...] a way
of fighting for a better world where injustice is impossible and
where man [...] advances, confident and secure, in search of
widespread perfection."[38] The protagonists of the last five works
struggle for this better world, striving to enlighten society about

the evils of social injustice, hypocrisy, and war. Esquilache institutes a series of reforms to cure his country of its stubborn blindness and to bring "light" to an agonizing people; Velázquez struggles to declare the truth and to paint the injustice, pretense, and hypocrisy of his epoch; and Goya, to depict the monstrous evil of his own. Silvano and Eloy both endeavor to impart their dreams of peace and reconciliation. A basic aim of Buero's theater is to overcome the fanaticism and sectarianism which have darkened Spain's history—the fratricidal rage of Goya's *Fighting with Clubs.*

For Buero, as for Galdós, this reconciliation may be accomplished only through the *misericordia* or compassion with which the neighbors in *Today's a Holiday* forgive the poor old woman who has sold them false shares of a lottery ticket. The families in tragedies such as *The Cards Face Down, Story of a Stairway,* and *The Basement Window,* with their petty conflicts and quarrels, their blind incomprehension and lack of generosity, are, in fact, microcosms of the society seen in the historical tragedies and the fantasies just discussed. For Pérez Minik, Buero's plays all represent, under various masks, a continuing trial in which Spanish history is brought to judgment.[39] The same message is heard in the words of Julián in *The Awaited Sign,* when he states that "perhaps we all have to forgive each other," and of Juan in *The Cards Face Down,,* when he comes to realize that "we are all innocent and culpable," as of Goya when he maintains that "we are none of us without guilt."

A fundamental affirmation of all Buero's theater is the necessity of the individual exercising his inviolable liberty by winning a victory over himself, by overcoming his innate egoism. The evidence of man's love for his fellow human beings must be his kindness and abnegation. As Borel points out, Buero's protagonists discover that life has meaning only through this love. Past culpability can be erased only through efforts on behalf of others; individual victory can be realized only in and through society.[40] Moreover, man's ethical concern—if he does not close his ears to human suffering like the Grandmother in *The Double Case History of Dr. Valmy*—must necessarily be translated into political activity. For Buero, even the activist and politician must be an altruistic dreamer like Esquilache.

Buero's dreamers, who strive to create the better world they envision, although morally superior to those around them, are derided as ingenuous or deluded idealists and madmen. Tragic heroes who strive to transform society into the image of their chosen ideal, they are defeated by a reality which seems unchangeable. We see the seemingly inevitable failure of human ideals and aspirations to change the world. In their struggle, however, they show their true greatness—their integrity and refusal to compromise.

In a lecture on the importance of Unamuno, Buero explains that the Spaniard usually interprets tragedy quixotically because, for centuries, his efforts have been thwarted by an inert society seemingly impermeable to change. "Therefore great geniuses become quixoticized, they assume a sort of lucid madness and evolve toward action that is seemingly—but only seemingly—sterile."[41] The madness of Don Quijote, Buero adds, is also the madness of Larra and Unamuno. For Buero, quixotism is not sterile because it is synonymous with individual integrity and responsibility.

All the plays in this chapter evince Buero's "lack of aesthetic satisfaction"[42] and his continuing search for appropriate techniques to express the problems of present-day society: historical distancing, fantasy, and music. Notable, especially, are the auditory and visual effects in the recreation of Goya's caprice in *The Sleep of Reason* and the daring, almost surrealistic dream of *Adventure in Grey* which is absolutely essential to the play's meaning. Buero's constant experimentation reaches a climax in *Myth*, a most unusual experience in Spanish theater, comparable to Brecht's efforts, in *The Threepenny Opera*, to create a new type of musical theater appropriate to contemporary times.

CHAPTER 7

Internal Victory versus External Defeat: The Tragic Sense of Life

"Those distant worlds are there . . . behind the window panes, within our sight . . . if we had it!"
—*En la ardiente oscuridad* (*In the Burning Darkness*)[1]

W HEREAS the tragedies which have been analyzed evince the social emphasis of Buero's theater, two others gravitate toward a metaphysical or philosophical pole. *En la ardiente oscuridad* (*In the Burning Darkness*), 1950, and *Irene o el tesoro* (*Irene or the Treasure*), 1954, represent a search for metaphysical "light" or understanding. Neither, however, lacks social significance, for all of man's problems, even when metaphysical in nature, possess social transcendence. Buero's entire theater is an effort to understand what he calls "the great miracle of reality."[2] Buero's metaphysical concern has been evident in the unique moment of peace and comprehension at the end of *The Awaited Sign*, the moment of special "clarity" experienced by Pilar in *Today's a Holiday* when the evil of the world seems to dissolve into insignificance, and in Velázquez' assertion that the light must represent the form of God if he has one.

I En la ardiente oscuridad (In the Burning Darkness)

While David's longing to see, in *The Concert at Saint Ovide*, represents his desire to overcome the physical obstacle to his self-realization as a musician, Ignacio's, in *In the Burning Darkness*, represents a longing for metaphysical truth. That Ignacio, being blind, merges his desire to overcome his physical handicap with his metaphysical anguish is obvious. For he knows that if he could see the stars, he would "die of grief" because he

137

"could not reach them" (p. 60). His preoccupation is quite similar to Velázquez', whose questions about the ultimate meaning of light, in his painting, are synonymous to his wonder about the ultimate meaning of reality.

In the Burning Darkness takes place in an institution for students who have been blind from birth, where the atmosphere is one of artificial laughter and optimism. In this pleasant refuge from the real world, the student leader, Carlos, and his friends study, laugh, joke, fall in love, and even marry. The world of these students, who are apparently so well adjusted to reality, is a world of illusion. In their self-deception and unwillingness to confront the reality of their situation, they refuse to acknowledge that they are blind. Taking solace in the illusion that they are normal, they even refer to those who can see as *videntes* or "sighted." The comfort which they find in this illusory and protected world of darkness is suggested by the stanza from Miguel Hernández' *Hijo de la sombra* (*Son of the Darkness*), which precedes the tragedy:

> Shadow has become the closed, incandescent nest—
> visible blindness setting upon the lover;
> it already provokes blindly the closed embrace,
> it enfolds in its caverns whatever light disdains.[3]

Isolated in their school, their world of shadows and darkness —a world which has often been compared to that of Plato's cave —they are ignorant of the light which shines outside. This idea is well expressed by Buero's other epigraph: "The light shineth in darkness, and the darkness comprehended it not" (John 1:5). Thus, *In the Burning Darkness* is really a metaphysical tragedy. In Buero's symbolism the institution represents this world, and the students, man in general who is spiritually blind. Buero has stated that he is depicting not the physically blind, but all of us.[4] This spiritual blindness is described by the playwright as "the blind and tranquil self-sufficiency of people from all walks of life facing their destiny, a self-sufficiency which leads us to believe we possess the truth when we are most in error, and through which we will be lost... if, first, we are not called painfully, to greater awareness."[5]

Ignacio, a new student, points out to the others the fiction and hypocrisy upon which their existence is based. The center, he maintains, is founded on the lie that they are normal. Their life is only a parody of what it could be if they could see, and to pretend otherwise is insincerity. "I can't restrain myself," he cries, "I can't leave people with lies when they ask me. . . . The self-deception in which they live horrifies me!" (p. 51). For him the meaning of life is found only through facing the truth without evasion. He insists to the students: "You have no right to live, because you refuse to suffer; because you refuse to confront your tragedy, by feigning a normality that doesn't exist, and by trying to forget" (p. 28). One critic of Buero's theater states the problem which we see in the tragedy as follows: "Does one best find the meaning of life by seeking illusion and forgetting one's intimate problem, or is it better to stick to reality . . . however harsh it may be?"[6] Laín Entralgo formulates the question thus: "Which is preferable, an existence of belief and illusions, without problems, which Kant called a 'dogmatic slumber,' or the uncertain and risky way of life which inexorably brings with it the opening of the soul's eyes to the hidden dangers and problems of earthly truth?"[7] "For Buero, as for Unamuno," Isabel Schevill states, "the tragedy of man, implicit in the knowledge and exercise of free will is preferable to the ignorance and complacency of spiritual blindness."[8] She points out that Buero's anguished protagonists torn between faith and doubt, as well as the theme of physical and spiritual blindness, also place the playwright in the tradition of Unamuno.

Ignacio's anguish is revealed most clearly when he points out the difference between himself and the other students: "You are too peaceful, too insincere, too cold. But I am burning inside; burning with a terrible fire that doesn't let me live . . . burning in what those with sight call darkness, which is horrifying because we don't know what it is." When asked by Juana, a fellow student, what it is of which he dreams, Ignacio replies: "To see! Although I know that it is impossible, to see! Although I consume my whole life uselessly in this desire. I want to see! I can't content myself. We cannot be content. And much less smile! And resign ourselves with your stupid joy of blind men, never!" (p. 30). In his Unamunian passion for the absolute, his desire to transcend the limitations of the human condition and to penetrate the mysteries of man and the universe, Ignacio obviously resembles Mario of *The Basement Window*.

For Ignacio, a dreamer like David, the world of the students, their "cavern" of shadows and blindness, is not the only world. "Haven't you noticed," he asks Carlos, "that the night is dry and cold? Don't you know what that means?... It means that now the stars are shining in all their splendor, and that people with sight enjoy the marvel of their presence. Those distant worlds are there ... behind the windowpanes, within our sight ... if we had it!" (pp. 59-60).

This message is ultimately one of hope, when interpreted symbolically. For if the blind students represent man in general, who has created a world in his own image and likeness, Ignacio is the mystic who brings to them the message of a transcendent world to which most men are spiritually blind. The tragedy of the students lies precisely in their failure to experience this hope, hope for the "light": "They say we are incurable," acknowledges Ignacio, "but can we be certain? No one knows what life has in store for us, from a scientific discovery ... to a miracle" (p. 60). As Ignacio knows, however, hope, if it is to be genuine, must be founded on an awareness of truth—the students' blindness—and consequently, of anguish. Ignacio's obsession with the light, in the words of one critic, represents "a desire to find some positive cause for hope based on the total acceptance of suffering."[9] Carlos' defense of the institution is symbolic of "the human blindness which prefers to perpetuate a comfortable fiction rather than accept the truth."[10]

When compared to Carlos and the other students, "who dream the vague and inconsistent dream of their illusions of normality," Ignacio, who dreams of the truths which he does not know, "seems a radical and intransigent realist."[11] However, Ignacio, like David, is a man of immense hope, whereas Carlos, despite his apparent optimism, is a skeptic and a fatalist. Like the blind beggars in *The Concert at Saint Ovide*, he is content to accept his limitations.

A rebel like David, Ignacio influences all surounding him, bringing "war and not peace." His militant, proselytizing zeal is, indeed, worthy of his namesake, the soldier of Loyola. In a climactic scene, he finally succeeds in making Carlos understand his anguish; and Buero, by means of a skillful stage effect, makes the spectator identify with the problem of his characters. As Ignacio explains to Carlos how people close their eyes to imagine the horror of blindness, the stage and house lights are extinguished, leaving only the light of the stars shining through the window. Then it, too, disappears, leaving the theater completely dark. Then, as Ignacio describes how people rejoice when the light returns in the morning, the stars begin to shine once again and the stage is once more illuminated. We have here the same skillful use of contrasting light and darkness on stage which has already been noted in the scene in which David kills the impresario. "Yes, I understand you," responds Carlos, "I understand you, but I can't excuse you. . . . You're . . . a deranged Messiah! I'll tell you what's wrong with you: You have a death-wish. You say you want to see. . . . What you want is to die!" "Perhaps . . . perhaps," answers Ignacio, "it may be that death is the only way to attain the definitive vision" (pp. 61-62).

Ignacio's influence gradually begins to be seen, not only in Carlos, but in the entire group of students, as the atmosphere of superficial optimism and gaiety becomes one of anguish. The tranquil blindness of the students turns into painful awareness as Ignacio succeeds in his aim, to awaken the sincerity of each one. The students' unhappiness is underscored by the change of the green foliage of the trees seen through the window in the first act to bare branches and dry leaves at the beginning of the second, and by the music played over the institution's loud-speaker, Beethoven's "Moonlight Sonata," which, according to legend, was inspired by a blind boy. "My words," Carlos points out to Ignacio, "may help our companions achieve a life that is relatively happy. Yours will bring only destruction, driving them to despair, making them abandon their studies" (p. 46).

The opposition between Ignacio and Carlos terminates in the murder of the former, when it is apparent to Carlos that Ignacio is destroying the students' morale. Ignacio's dreams, however, live on in his murderer. For Carlos, no longer content with his artificial world of darkness, is, in the end, convinced that there exists another, more authentic world symbolized by the distant stars. Standing beside Ignacio's body, he repeats some of his very words: "Those distant worlds are there . . . within our sight! . . . if only we had it" (p. 77). No longer able to deceive himself, Carlos will live with Ignacio's despair, but also with his hope. The survival of Ignacio's ardent longings is dramatically represented by the presence of his body on stage during much of the third act.

Truth and the acceptance of suffering provide the basis upon which Carlos and the other students may found a positive hope in a more authentic world of "light." It has been remarked that in Buero's tragedies, "once the truth has been confronted, the ground is cleared for the possibility of a solution, for some kind of genuine hope."[12] There is a basis for hope not only for the "light," but moreover for the attainment of a more authentic form of existence which will result from the conflict between reason and faith. We may compare a similar idea expressed by Unamuno: "But here, in the depths of the abyss, heartfelt, willful despair and rational skepticism meet face to face and embrace like brothers. And it is out of this embrace, a tragic—that is to say, an intimately loving—embrace, that will flow the wellspring of life, a serious and terrible life."[13] Man must admit his blindness and suffering, the dramatist implies, so that he may, at least, find the consolation of a love born of mutual compassion and generosity, a love such as Ignacio sought with Juana, for whose affections he becomes a rival with Carlos. Indeed, the two students' rivalry over her lends greater verisimilitude to their ideological struggle, as is also the case with David, Valindin, and Adriana. Ignacio came to the institution, he told Juana, looking for a woman capable of sharing his anguish and his hope . . . not someone deluded.

Hope seems justified, as Carlos, even before the death of Ignacio, finally admits that life is harsh and bitter, and yet still believes that it is worth living: "I defend life! . . . Because I want to live it completely, to carry out its purpose; although it may not be peaceful or happy. Although it may be harsh and bitter. . . . Life has something to offer, it asks something of us, it has a claim on us" (p. 62). "Tragedy," according to Buero, "accepts the darker side of life and, on the basis of that acceptance, tries to deduce a positive attitude to human problems."[14]

It is only after the death of Ignacio that the real drama begins: "Only momentarily," Buero comments, "is there realized on stage the tragic reconciliation with Carlos, who inherits—because he always carried it in his heart, for he is an Ignacio who fights against being one—the preoccupations of the dead

youth. But if Carlos and his school succeed some day in recon-
ciling the limited optimism which they feel collectively with the
higher summons of their individuality, Ignacio, who was sacri-
ficed beneath the stars which he professed, will be the distant
promoter of the new reality attained."[15]

II   Irene ó el tesoro (Irene or the Treasure)

In *Irene or the Treasure,* subtitled a "fable," we have the same
contrast between this world of shadows and the protagonist's
dreams of a new world of "light" which we saw in *In the Burning Darkness.* The world represented in the last tragedy by the
institution for the blind is represented here by a sad house,
inhabited, for the most part, by "poor beings who live and
breathe their wretchedness, without even suspecting the mystery that surrounds them."[16] In this sordid, gray world, comparable to the "cavern" of darkness in the last play, lives Irene,
a sad and disillusioned widow who lost her only son at child-
birth and who is now abused and treated as a domestic servant
by her dead husband's family.

When Irene is alone, she sings and dreams of the child for
whom she yearns: "When I sing the lullaby, I see him better.
I know what he would have been like. With curly hair, blue eyes
and a mischievous smile. He would have been. . . . My beloved
son! Like a little elf! [. . .] But the darkness overpowers me"
(p. 30). In this world of "blackness," Irene, like Ignacio, dreams
of a new world of light: "My God . . . lighten this horrible darkness and give me what is mine" (p. 42). And, in effect, there
appears one day a "little elf," Juanito, sent to find a hidden treasure. Juanito is both a compensation for Irene's frustrated mother-
hood and the incarnation of the world of "light" and "clarity"
for which Irene yearns—the world represented in *In the Burning
Darkness* by the distant stars for which Ignacio longs. For at
the command of the mysterious Voice which directs his actions,
Juanito twirls his magic pick and Irene's world of darkness is
filled with brilliant red, blue, and orange lights. He then tells
Irene to open the balcony; and, instead of "rooftops and cats,"
there is seen "a miracle of bright white light. It resembles a
slightly sloping corridor which reaches the balcony, with its
strange and oddly shaped walls of a diamond-like brightness"
(pp. 62-63).

144 ANTONIO BUERO VALLEJO

Irene is the only one in the house who sees Juanito and the lights, for the other members of the family are as spiritually blind as are the students of *In the Burning Darkness* and the members of the royal household in *Almost a Fairy Tale,* who cannot see the handsome prince. They are as unaware of the mystery beyond their grasp as the actors in *Myth* who are incapable of hearing the music of the helmet. For a moment, however, it seems that a poor youth who rooms in the house may be able to share Irene's world. In his words we see clearly the antirationalistic attitude which is a major characteristic of all of Buero's theater:

DANIEL: Of what value is reason? The deceitful reason of this prosaic world may be a great madness. (*She moves.*) Don't be frightened! Words don't mean anything. The same as reason, more or less. It is our feelings which save us.
[. . . .]
You know that I'm only a poor dreamer. And we dreamers, all know that the world isn't only this sordid reality that surrounds us, that there is also, even though it may not seem like it, a permanent and mysterious marvel which envelops us.
IRENE: There is, isn't there?
DANIEL: Yes. And that marvel keeps watch over us and permeates our lives. . . . And perhaps some day we'll be able to see it face to face.
IRENE: (*Excited.*) Face to face. . . . Daniel! But, no. You can't understand.
DANIEL: I'll understand everything you want me to. When I studied, I understood St. Theresa and St. John of the Cross. They lived in a world where marvelous things happened too. . . . They were called mad. And they were really saints.

Juanito and the Voice represent this new reality of "light," the world for which Ignacio longed. Of course, they may be only hallucinations of the protagonist, whom the other characters consider insane. Indeed, the doctor who is sent for states that definitive proof of Irene's insanity would be a hallucination. He even goes so far as to suggest that if Don Quijote, being a man, saw giants to combat, Irene, being a woman, may see an elf or a child to kiss. Thus, the Voice of Juanito may exist only in the protagonist's imagination. The Voice, itself, ironically suggests this in a subtly humorous dialogue after Juanito expresses his alarm at the doctor's words:

JUANITO: In the midst of all this, it's a consolation to hear you. It's proof that I exist.
THE VOICE: No, my son. That doesn't prove anything.
[...]
Human minds are very complicated. They all have a big basement, where a lot of intelligence is stored. And you may have come out of that basement. . . . That is so true that even stupid human doctors have found out about its existence.
JANITO: About the basement?
THE VOICE: Yes. And they call it the subconscious. (p. 92)

Of course, we have seen in *The Basement Window* that the hallucinations of the mad father constitute a new access to reality. In like manner, it is possible that Irene reaches a spiritual reality which the others, in their sanity, are unable to attain.

Indeed, when Juanito begins to question his own reality because he is seen only by Irene, the Voice, after playing with his doubts as if to test his faith, affirms the existence of both. The reality of "light" which they represent, it is implied, is the true one.

JUANITO: I believe that you are God.
THE VOICE: Get up [from your knees] and don't pronounce that word. It's too elevated for all of us.
JUANITO: (*Gets up.*) Who are you? (*Silence.*) Are you an angel? (*Silence.*) Tell me if all this is true. Tell me if I am true and if you are, because only then will I believe that she isn't mad.
THE VOICE: The wisdom of men is madness, and their madness can be wisdom.
JUANITO: Then, everything is true? I'm not deceived?
THE VOICE: For the insane wisdom of men, you and I are a delusion. But the world has two faces. . . . And from ours, which encompasses the other, emanates reality! This is the true reality. (p. 110)

The entire tragedy or fable, Buero has pointed out, is based upon an equivocation.[17] The mere fact that the Voice affirms their existence does not mean that they are real. Juanito may represent Irene's reason, her doubts; and the Voice, her faith, both of which, Buero comments, "are living the tragedy of their own existence and struggle to survive"—the same Unamunian struggle which we saw in Ignacio. Obviously the fact that the elf is

perceived by the audience does not mean that it must be real—
any more than the melody of the helmet in *Myth* or the mysterious music at the end of *The Awaited Sign*.
The equivocation continues to the end. When the doctor comes,
we are surprised to see that it is Dimas himself, who is taken
away to the asylum, since the family has convinced the former
that Dimas' avarice is pathological. Juanito, told by the Voice
that Irene herself, who represents "the gold of kindness," is the
treasure which he has been sent to find, urges her to come to
his land where happiness awaits her. At the end of the tragedy
we see Irene, her face transfigured with joy, move slowly away
on the miraculous path of light outside the balcony. Irene, whose
flight represents a sort of rebellion against the darkness, may
have reached a world of "diamond-like brightness," the world
symbolized in *In the Burning Darkness* by the stars. A poor,
simpleminded woman, she may have reached the world for
which Ignacio longed but could not find—perhaps because she
represents "kindness." It is not reason, but "feeling" which
saves us, Daniel has stated. Irene, in short, may have realized
her dreams. The epigraph for the tragedy is two lines from
Unamuno's *Cancionero* or *Collection of Songs*: "The secret
of the soul redeemed: to live one's dreams as life is dreamed"
—verses which express a major idea of all of Buero's theater.
On the other hand, Irene may have only succumbed to a
hallucination. For, as we hear her lullaby and see her move
away on the path of light, we also hear the shouts of the other
characters who see her dead body on the cobblestones below.
By maintaining this equivocation, the playwright hopes to "make
man think and to demonstrate that things never have a single
perspective."[18] Multifaceted in the levels of reality it presents
and the questions it raises, the tragedy is ambivalent but in no
sense pessimistic.

Irene's dreams of escaping from the sordid reality about her
to a world of brilliant clarity parallel Ignacio's yearning to
reach a trascendent world symbolized by the distant stars—the
new world where Penelope professes her faith that she will some
day go to meet Anfino, who awaits her. In both tragedies there is
suggested, although not confirmed, the possibility of man's
reaching the "light."

José Luis Abellán comments that Buero's plays may be viewed as a consistent effort to "open up for us a pathway toward the light"—even knowing that it may not be possible to reach it—"an attempt to open a sphere of transcendence to human life."[19] "Buero," he adds, "is an exceptional Spanish playwright in that, without ceasing to be relevant and to assume the existential problematics of man, he does not lose himself in a pessimism without exit." Rosendo Roig, in an article on tragic elements in Buero's theater,[20] and Carlos Muñiz, in a study of religious symbolism,[21] both emphasize the Christian existential nature of the search for "light" in his theater. "Buero asks a question," states the former, "convinced that the answer will be another query. [. . .] And, if, in spite of everything he goes on writing—and searching—it is in the hope that each question will be clearer and the answer, nearer. Buero Vallejo's theater is, therefore, tragic." In reference to *Irene or the Treasure*, Buero himself states that "the most positive consequence of the drama is the affirmation of the reality of mystery as such and of its profound relationship with that other commonplace reality in which our everyday existence takes place."[22] His purpose, he continues, is "to revitalize our spirit [. . .] by raising some of the questions which accompany us through life rather than muffle them with strict affirmations."

In the two plays last discussed, as in most of Buero's theater, the metaphysical is intermingled with the social. It is not only his blindness—both physical and spiritual—against which Ignacio rebels, but the attitude of society which minimizes its significance. Irene's dreams likewise represent a judgment upon the other characters. Her longing for a new reality of light is, in a sense, an escape from the death of her baby when Dimas refused to spend money for necessary medicine, and from the abuse to which she is subjected in the miser's house—just as the father's madness in *The Basement Window* represents a refuge from the egoism responsible for his baby daughter's death years before. Here, as in most of Buero's tragedies, we see the contrast between man's egoism and his kindness. In its exposition of social realities, *Irene or the Treasure* obviously resembles *Story of a Stairway* and *Today's a Holiday*, which depict the misery and sordidness of the existence of the lower economic classes. This sordidness of Irene's surroundings is indeed underscored by its contrast with the new world of "light" that she dreams of.

Both *In the Burning Darkness* and *Irene or the Treasure* exemplify the same sort of symbolic realism we have seen in many of Buero's plays, such as *The Awaited Sign* and *Today's a Holiday*, which, also, have metaphysical or transcendent elements. In *Irene or the Treasure*, we have a lyric and poetic atmosphere quite similar to that of *The Awaited Sign, Almost a Fairy Tale*, and *The Dream Weaver*. The visual and auditory effects so noted by critics in Buero's recent works, such as *The Sleep of Reason*, are not absent from these plays even though *In the Burning Darkness* is the first play he wrote and *Irene or the Treasure* among his earliest. The visual contrast of the green leaves with the bare tree branches in *In the Burning Darkness*—which reminds us that Buero, like several of his characters, was once a painter—sets the anguished tone of the play in much the same way as the music of "Moonlight Sonata" and "Aase's Death" from the *Peer Gynt Suite*, which is heard when Ignacio is murdered. The lullaby which Irene hums when she dreams of her child recalls the violin music which David of *The Concert at Saint Ovide* plays whenever he dreams of Melania, symbol of the ideal, and Handel's "Water Music," which sounds whenever Leticia of *Almost a Fairy Tale* sees the ugly Prince Riquet through the eyes of love. Indeed, the skillful use of music, which reaches a climax in *Myth*, is a major characteristic of all of Buero's theatrical works.

CHAPTER 8

Conclusion

F ROM the time of the ancient Greeks to that of contemporary dramatists, tragedy is often viewed as man's search for truth or understanding about himself and the universe; and it is in this way that the tragic theater of Buero Vallejo may perhaps be best understood. Buero Vallejo's protagonists are often—although not always—rebellious dreamers or idealists who strive to transcend the limitations of the human condition. Some struggle for the truth or understanding which will permit them to realize their human potential to the fullest, others for the understanding which will permit them to find a metaphysical basis for life. Some plays evince the social emphasis of the playwright's theater and others gravitate toward a metaphysical pole. These two searches for truth, however, are not mutually exclusive. To express this quest for knowledge, Buero often uses a double metaphor: light and darkness, vision and blindness. In his theater, "light" represents any sort of comprehension which can help man overcome his limitations.

Buero believes that hope is an essential element of tragedy; to be genuine, however, hope must be based upon truth. Only after the truth of man's situation has been sought and confronted —however dark it may be—is there the possibility of any real solution to human problems. In view of the usual statements that tragedy is pessimistic and negative, he believes that "it is important to elucidate the paradoxical truth which justifies the genre: it is [tragedy] which seeks the true foundations of a possible human optimism which is not based on illusion, deceit, or blindness. It is the most hopeful genre, despite its description of hopelessness."[1]

In their struggle for understanding, Buero's protagonists are seen as torn between their limitations and their desires, between doubt and faith, reality and dreams. More mystical than rational,

149

they often strive for the seemingly impossible. We have seen, however, that, for Buero, tragedy represents a conflict between "liberty" (or free will) and "necessity" (or human limitations), which is not inexorably resolved in favor of the latter.

Most of Buero's tragedies conclude with the external defeat of the protagonist. Penelope, Silverio, Juan, David, Silvano, Eloy, Esquilache, Goya, Ignacio, and others are defeated by their circumstances. Many, however, win an internal victory through their integrity and refusal to compromise. As is the case in all tragedy, moreover, their outward defeat implies the survival of their inner ideals and hopes, which live on in those whom they have influenced—Fernandita, symbol of the common people in whom Esquilache expresses his faith, or Carlos, the student leader who will live with Ignacio's dreams of a transcendent reality of "light." Often hope lies with the new generation—Juanito, whom his father allows to leave home to study abroad in order that he may avoid his parents' mistakes; the baby saved by Silvano and Ana, or Encarna's child whom Mario agrees to adopt as his own in *The Basement Window*. There is implied the possibility that they may succeed in creating the better world that their parents were unable to.

Buero's tragedies generally end ambivalently with a question the purpose of which is to lead the spectator to reflect upon the problems presented. However, even the tragedy ending in catastrophe without apparent hope, such as *The Words in the Sand*, invites him to avoid the mistakes of the protagonist; for Buero believes that theater ends not with the final scene, but with the possible spiritual ennoblement of the spectator.

From an analysis of Buero's plays, it is obvious that he has followed very closely his own concept of tragedy as a phenomenon which is always positive, which proposes an encounter with the truth which may free man from his spiritual blindness. His plays propose this encounter, but they do not affirm it. Therefore, his attitude toward this struggle for truth which his tragedies propose, is hardly the "resounding 'yes'" for which he says the writer of tragedy longs.[2] Since most of them end with a question rather than any definitive solution, his attitude is rather one of unending hope, that heralded by doña Nieves in *Today's a Holiday*: "One must hope ... always hope. ... Hope never ends. Hope is infinite."[3]

Notes and References

Chapter One

1. Ed. José Janés (Barcelona, 1950), p. 153.
2. See Juan Emilio Aragonés, "El teatro español y su encrucijada," *Bolívar*, Nos. 41-45 (Bogotá, 1955), p. 509. See also Gonzalo Torrente Ballester, "Teatro de evasión," in *Teatro español contemporáneo* (Madrid, 1957), pp. 194-208.
3. Buero, "El teatro como problema," *Almanaque de teatro y cine* (Madrid, 1951), p. 58.
4. See Buero, "Cuidado con la amargura," *Correo Literario*, No. 2 (June 15, 1950), p. 8.
5. Juan del Sarto, "Buero Vallejo considera . . . ," *Correo Literario*, No. 52 (July 15, 1952), p. 3.
6. Arcadio Baquero, "Buero Vallejo, pintor," *La Estafeta Literaria*, No. 198 (August, 1960), p. 15.
7. Buero, "El teatro de Buero Vallejo visto por Buero Vallejo," *Primer Acto*, No. 1 (April, 1957), p. 5.
8. Carlos Fernández Cuenca, "En sólo una semana escribió Buero Vallejo la primera versión de *En la ardiente oscuridad*," *Correo Literario*, No. 69 (1953), pp. 10-12.
9. Alfredo Marqueríe, "Prólogo," *Historia de una escalera*, ed. José Janés (Barcelona, 1950), p. 8.
10. Juan Emilio Aragonés, "Antonio Buero Vallejo, académico," *La Estafeta Literaria*, No. 462 (February 15, 1971), p. 9.
11. See, for example, Buero, "Habla Buero Vallejo para 'Faro de Vigo,'" *Faro de Vigo* (January 16, 1960), pp. 7-8.
12. Medardo Fraile, "Charla con Antonio Buero Vallejo," *Cuadernos de Agora*, Nos. 79-82 (May-August, 1963), p. 8.
13. Fernández Cuenca, pp. 10-12.
14. Buero, "El teatro como problema," *Almanaque* . . . , p. 58.
15. Quoted in Carlos Muñiz, S.J., "El simbolismo religioso en el teatro de Buero Vallejo," *Proyección*, No. 37 (Granada, April, 1963).
16. Rosendo Roig, S.J., "Talante trágico del teatro de Buero Vallejo," *Razón y Fe*, No. 156 (Madrid, 1957), p. 364.
17. José Luis Abellán, "El tema del misterio en Buero Vallejo, (Un teatro de la realidad trascendente)," *Insula*, No. 174 (May 15, 1961), p. 15.

Chapter Two

1. Madrid: Ediciones Alfil, 1957, pp. 99-100.
2. Buero, "Sobre la tragedia," *Entretiens sur les Lettres et les Arts*, No. 22 (Rodez, France, 1963), p. 57.
3. Buero, "Comentario," *En la ardiente oscuridad* (Madrid: Ediciones Alfil, 1951), p. 83.
4. Buero, "Ibsen y Ehrlich," *Informaciones* (April 4, 1953).
5. Buero Vallejo, "La tragedia," *El teatro; enciclopedia del arte escénico*, ed. Guillermo Díaz-Plaja (Barcelona: Editorial Noguer, S.A., 1958), p. 67.
6. *Ibid.*, p. 71.
7. *Ibid.*, p. 85.
8. "Antonio Buero Vallejo Answers Seven Questions," *Theater Annual* (1962), p. 5.
9. Buero, "Comentario," *La señal que se espera* (Madrid: Ediciones Alfil, 1953), pp. 66-67.
10. Buero, "Sobre teatro," *Cuadernos de Agora*, Nos. 79-82 (May-August, 1963), pp. 12-14.
11. José R. Marra-López, "Conversación con Antonio Buero Vallejo," *Cuadernos del Congreso por la Libertad de la Cultura*, No. 42 (May-June, 1960), p. 56.
12. Buero, "Antonio Buero Vallejo Answers Seven Questions." See note 8.
13. Buero Vallejo, "Sobre la tragedia," *Entretiens* . . . . See note 2.
14. Buero, "La tragedia," *El teatro; enciclopedia* . . . , p. 74.
15. *Ibid.* Also, Buero, "Palabra final," *Historia de una escalera*, ed. José Janés (Barcelona, 1950), p. 154.
16. Buero, "Teatro anodino: teatro escandaloso," *Informaciones* (March 24, 1951).
17. Buero, "La tragedia," *El teatro; enciclopedia* . . . ., pp. 74-75.
18. Buero, "Sobre teatro," p. 13. See note 10.
19. Buero, "Me llamo Antonio Buero Vallejo," *Discos Aguilar* (Madrid, 1964), side B.

Buero has explained that when his early plays were attacked as "pessimistic," he reacted polemically, speaking of them as "optimistic." He now prefers the word "hopeful." His theater, he states, is one in which "the most pessimistic aspects of man and his circumstances are not denied or hidden, but which does not postulate fate or negativity as the ultimate significance of life. There is then the dialectical presumption of both [pessimism and optimism] in the sense that the tragic is ultimately hopeful."

Cf. Gonzalo Pérez de Olaguer, "Antonio Buero Vallejo, nuevo académico de la lengua," *Yorick*, No. 46 (March, 1971), p. 8.

20. Buero, "Palabra final," *Historia de una escalera* (Barcelona, 1950), p. 155.

21. Buero Vallejo, "Comentario," *Irene o el tesoro* (Madrid: Ediciones Alfil, 1955), pp. 122-23.

22. Medardo Fraile, "Charla con Antonio Buero Vallejo," *Cuadernos de Agora*, Nos. 79-82 (May-August, 1963), p. 5.

23. Buero, "El teatro de Buero Vallejo visto por Buero Vallejo," *Primer Acto*, No. 1 (April, 1957), p. 6. See also Gonzalo Pérez de Olaguer, p. 9.

24. Buero, "Antonio Buero Vallejo habla de Unamuno," *Primer Acto*, No. 59 (November, 1964), pp. 19-21.

25. Bernard Dulsey, "Entrevista a Buero Vallejo," *The Modern Language Journal*, L, No. 3 (March, 1966), 153.

26. *Ibid.*

27. Brustein, *The Theater of Revolt* (Boston: Little, Brown and Co., 1962), pp. 24-25.

28. Buero, "Sobre teatro," *Cuadernos de Agora*, No. 79-82 (Barcelona, May-June, 1963), p. 13.

29. Buero, "Comentario," *Hoy es fiesta* (Madrid: Ediciones Alfil, 1957), p. 102.

30. Buero, "A propósito de Brecht," *Ínsula*, XVIII, Nos. 200-201 (July-August, 1963), 1-14.

31. *Ibid.*, 14.

32. Buero, "Sobre teatro," *Cuadernos de Agora*, Nos. 79-82 (May-August, 1963), p. 13.

33. *Ibid.*, pp. 13-14.

34. See Buero, "De rodillas, en pie, en el aire (Sobre el autor y sus personajes en el teatro de Valle-Inclán)," *Revista de Occidente*, XV (1966), 132-45.

35. Buero, "La tragedia," *El teatro; enciclopedia . . . .*, p. 77.

36. Buero, "Comentario," *Hoy es fiesta*, p. 100. See note 29.

37. *Ibid.*

38. "El teatro de Buero Vallejo visto por Buero Vallejo," p. 6. See note 23.

39. Gonzalo Pérez de Olaguer, pp. 8-9.

40. Buero, *El teatro; enciclopedia . . .*, p. 77.

41. *Ibid.*

42. *Ibid.*, p. 76.

43. *Ibid.*, pp. 86-87.

44. Louis Martz, "The Saint as Tragic Hero," *Tragic Themes in Western Literature*, ed. Cleanth Brooks (New Haven: Yale University Press, 1955), pp. 176-77.

45. Buero, *El teatro; enciclopedia . . .*, p. 77.

46. *Ibid.*, pp. 76-78. Also, Buero, "La ceguera en mi teatro," *La Carreta*, No. 12 (Barcelona, September, 1963), p. 5.

47. Dulsey, p. 154.

48. "Buero Vallejo y José Tamayo hablan del teatro en Hispanoamérica," *Correo Literario*, No. 33 (October, 1951), p. 3.

49. Buero, "La tragedia," *El teatro; enciclopedia* . . . , p. 84.

50. Buero, "Norrealismo y teatro," *Informaciones* (April 8, 1950).

51. Buero, "La tragedia," *El teatro; enciclopedia* . . . , p. 82.

52. Buero, "Buero Vallejo nos habla," *Negro sobre Blanco*, No. 12 (Buenos Aires: Editorial Losada S.A., April, 1960), p. 2. Buero's strong defense of a "closed" technique early in his career stemmed partially from the dangers he saw in an increased cultivation of the "open" technique to the exclusion of the former and from the belief that the "open" technique was designed mainly to attract the public from the cinema by imitating its devices when actually, the only way to win the battle against the cinema was by maintaining the theater's purity and integrity: by emphasizing "dialogue, a realistic construction which accepts, rather than avoids, the presentation of life in acts condensed in continuous periods of time, and only the action which such periods permit or can suggest." Buero, "Comentario," *Madrugada* (Madrid: Ediciones Alfil, 1954), pp. 84-87.

53. Buero, "Problemas del teatro actual," *Boletín de la Sociedad General de Autores de España* (April-May-June, 1970), pp. 31-32. This is the text of a speech Buero delivered in Las Palmas in 1971.

54. Julio Trenas, "Buero Vallejo, en y ante el teatro moderno," *ABC* (June 8, 1969).

55. Buero, "Problemas del teatro actual," pp. 32-34. See note 53.

56. *Ibid.*, p. 34.

57. *Ibid.*

58. For the comments of Lavelli and Planchon, see their interviews at the Avignon Theater Festival of 1967 published in *Primer Acto*, No. 91 (December, 1967), pp. 68-74.

59. Buero, "Problemas del teatro actual," p. 36.

60. *Ibid.*, p. 35.

61. Miguel Luis Rodríguez, "Diálogo con Antonio Buero Vallejo," *Índice*, XII, Nos. 116-17 (September-October, 1958), 21.

62. Buero, "Comentario," *En la ardiente oscuridad*, p. 82. See note 3.

63. Rodríguez, p. 21.

64. *Ibid.*

65. Miguel Luis Rodríguez, "Diálogo con Antonio Buero Vallejo," *Índice*, No. 118 (October, 1958), 22-23.

66. Buero, "Realism in 1965," *World Theatre*, XIV, No. 2 (1965), 154.

Chapter Three

1. Madrid: Ediciones Alfil, 1952, p. 72.
2. Buero, "Comentario," *En la ardiente oscuridad* (Madrid: Ediciones Alfil, 1951), p. 80.
3. Buero, "La ceguera en mi teatro," *La Carreta*, No. 12 (September, 1963), p. 5.
4. Buero, "Sobre la tragedia," *Entretiens sur les Lettres et les Arts*, No. 22 (France, 1963), p. 53.
5. Isabel M. de Schevill, "Lo trágico en el teatro de Buero Vallejo," *Hispanófila*, No. 1 (September, 1959), p. 55.
6. Buero, *En la ardiente oscuridad*, p. 28.
7. Cleanth Brooks, "Introduction," *Tragic Themes in Western Literature* (New Haven: Yale University Press, 1955), p. 5.
8. Buero, "Sobre la tragedia," *Entretiens* ..., No. 22, p. 55.
9. Buero, "La ceguera en mi teatro," *La Carreta*. See note 3.
10. Buero, "La tragedia," *El teatro; enciclopedia del arte escénico* (Barcelona: Editorial Noguer, S.A., 1958), p. 68.
11. See, for example, St. Jerome, *Dialogus contra Pelagianos*, Book II.
12. "Comentario," *Historia de una escalera y Las palabras en la arena* (Madrid: Ediciones Alfil, 1952), p. 86. All subsequent references are to this edition.
13. Buero uses this term to describe Carlos of *In the Burning Darkness*, but it is appropriate to many of his characters. Buero, "Comentario," *En la ardiente oscuridad*, pp. 82-83.
14. Buero, "Comentario," *Historia de una escalera* ..., p. 104.
15. *Ibid.*, p. 103.
16. *Ibid.*
17. Ángel Valbuena Prat, *Historia del teatro español* (Barcelona: Editorial Noguer, S.A., 1956), p. 662.
18. Buero, "Comentario," *La tejedora de sueños* (Madrid: Ediciones Alfil, 1952), pp. 78-85.
19. Buero, *La tejedora de sueños*, p. 66.
20. *Ibid.*, p. 79.
21. *Ibid.*, pp. 79-80.
22. J. E. Lyon, "Introduction," *Hoy es fiesta* (London: George G. Harrap & Co. Ltd., 1964), p. 22.
23. This tragedy has been called by Giménez Caballero, "the most Calderonian drama since the death of Calderón." Quoted by Rafael Suárez Solís in "El teatro español quiere modernizarse," *Diario de la Marina* (Havana, February 16, 1952), p. 4.
24. Buero, "Comentario," *Casi un cuento de hadas* (Madrid: Ediciones Alfil, 1953), p. 74.

25. Beth Noble, "Sound in the Plays of Buero Vallejo," *Hispania*, XLI, No. 1 (March, 1958), 57.

26. "Comentario," *Casi un cuento de hadas*, pp. 74-78.

27. *Ibid.*, p. 77.

28. *Ibid.*

29. Eduardo Haro Tecglen, "*Casi un cuento de hadas* de Antonio Buero Vallejo," *Informaciones* (January 2, 1953), p. 5.

30. Lyon, p. 25.

31. Jean-Paul Borel, *El teatro de lo imposible* (Madrid: Ediciones Guadarrama, 1966), p. 251.

32. Buero, *La tejedora de sueños*, p. 38.

33. Buero, "Autocrítica" to *Irene o el tesoro*, in *Teatro español 1954-55* ed. Sáinz de Robles (Madrid: Aguilar, 1958), pp. 21-22.

34. Miguel Luis Rodríguez, "Diálogo con Antonia Buero Vallejo," *Índice*, No. 119 (December, 1958), 20.

Chapter Four

1. Madrid: Ediciones Alfil, 1960, p. 96.

2. Buero, "Comentario," *Madrugada* (Madrid: Ediciones Alfil, 1954), p. 92.

3. Isabel Magaña de Schevill, "Introducción," *Dos dramas de Buero Vallejo* (New York: Appleton-Century-Crofts, 1967), p. 9.

4. Francis Fergusson, "*Ghosts*," in *Discussions of Henrik Ibsen*, ed. James McFarlane (Boston, 1962), p. 40.

5. José María de Quinto, "Crónica de la quincena," *Correo Literario* (January 1, 1954), p. 10.

6. Quoted by Buero, "Comentario," *Madrugada*, pp. 90-91.

7. *Ibid.*

8. Schevill, p. 10.

9. A[lfonso] S[astre], Review of "*Madrugada*," *Cuadernos Hispanoamericanos* (February, 1954), pp. 284-85.

10. Ibsen's ideas on inherited diseases were, of course, typical of his epoch.

11. Buero Vallejo, "La tragedia," *El teatro; enciclopedia del arte escénico* (Barcelona: Editorial Noguer, S.A., 1958), p. 76.

12. Buero subtitled the play *comedia dramática*. However, after writing the play, it became evident to him that, in the guise of a *comedia sentimental*, it is really *un relato trágico*. "Comentario," *La señal que se espera* (Madrid: Ediciones Alfil, 1952), pp. 66-67.

13. This music, a melody by Buero, is played by guitar.

14. Buero, "La tragedia," *El teatro; enciclopedia . . .* , p. 73.

15. Buero, "Comentario," *La señal que se espera*, p. 67.

16. *Ibid.*, pp. 67-68.

17. Buero's use of music in this play has been carefully analyzed by Angelo A. Borrás in his article "A note on Buero Vallejo's *La señal que se espera*," *Romance Notes*, XI, No. 2 (1970), 501-4.

18. Abellán, "El tema del misterio en Buero Valleo," *Insula*, No. '174 (May, 1961), p. 15.

19. Buero, *Hoy es fiesta* (Madrid: Ediciones Alfil, 1960, pp. 67-69.

20. Buero, "Comentario," *Hoy es fiesta*, p. 103.

21. Borel, *El teatro de lo imposible* (Madrid: Ediciones Guadarrama, 1966), p. 257.

22. Luis Ardilla, Review of *Hoy es fiesta*, from *Pueblo*, reprinted in *Teatro español 1956-57*, ed. Sáinz de Robles (Madrid: Aguilar, 1958), p. 41.

23. Borel, p. 179. See also J. F. Lyon, "Introduction," *Hoy es fiesta* (London: George G. Harrap & Co. Ltd., 1964), p. 34.

24. Buero, "Comentario," *Hoy es fiesta*, p. 103.

25. Enrique Sordo, Review of *Las cartas boca abajo*, from *Revista*, reprinted in *Teatro español 1957-58*, ed. Sáinz de Robles (Madrid: Aguilar, 1959), p. 6.

26. Buero, *Las cartas boca abajo* (Madrid: Ediciones Alfil, 1962), p. 32.

27. Felipe Bernardos, Review of *Las cartas boca abajo* from *Amanecer*, reprinted in *Teatro español 1957-58*, p. 8.

28. Francisco de Cossío, "El monólogo en el teatro," *ABC* (November 29, 1957), p. 3.

29. Sáinz de Robles, "Una crítica mía," *Teatro español 1957-58* (Madrid: Aguilar, 1959), pp. xvi-xx.

30. Sordo, p. 6.

31. Francisco Fernández-Santos, "*Las cartas boca abajo* de Buero Vallejo," *Índice*, No. 108 (January, 1958), 17.

32. Buero, *La doble historia del Doctor Valmy* in *Artes Hispánicas*, I, No. 2 (Autumn, 1967), 115. Translations are from the English text by Farris Anderson published in the same issue, and page numbers refer to the English.

33. Lyon, "Introduction," *Hoy es fiesta* (London: George G. Harrap & Co. Ltd., 1964), p. 38.

34. J[osé] M[aría] S[ouvirón], "Teatro, verdad, y poesía," *Papeles de Son Armadans*, III, No. 8 (November, 1956), 229.

35. Schevill, p. 1.

36. See Buero, "Una baraja en tres posturas," *La Estafeta Literaria*, No. 105 (November 23, 1967), p. 9.

37. Rafael Vázquez Zamora, "*Las cartas boca abajo* de Buero Vallejo," *Insula*, No. 134 (January 15, 1958), p. 15.

38. *Ibid*.

Chapter Five

1. Buero, *Historia de una escalera y Las palabras en la arena* (Madrid: Ediciones Alfil, 1952), p. 70.

2. Lyon, "Introduction," *Hoy es fiesta* (London: George G. Harrap and Co. Ltd., 1964), p. 36.

3. Alfredo Marquerie, Review of *Historia de una escalera* from *ABC*, reprinted in *Teatro español 1949-50*, ed. Sáinz de Robles (Madrid, 1951), p. 95.

4. See, for example, José Sánchez, Review of *Historia de una escalera* in *Books Abroad* (Autumn, 1951), p. 376.

5. Buero, "Cuidado con la amargura," *Correo Literario*, No. 2 (June 15, 1950), p. 8.

6. Arturo del Hoyo, "Sobre *Historia de una escalera*," *Insula*, No. 47 (November 15, 1949), p. 1. Fear of passing time is the major theme, also, of Buero's *El terror inmóvil; fragmentos de una tragedia irrepresentable*, the second act of which is published in *Número 100* (Ediciones Alfil, 1954), pp. 25-44.

7. Buero, "Palabra final," *Historia de una escalera*, ed. José Janés (Barcelona, 1950), p. 156.

8. Marquerie, p. 95.

9. del Hoyo, p. 1.

10. Robert Kirsner, "*Historia de una escalera*: A Play in Search of Characters," *Homenaje a Rodríguez Moñino*, I (1966), 281.

11. David William Foster, "*Historia de una escalera*: A Tragedy of Aboulia," *Renascence*, XVII (Fall, 1964), 9.

12. Buero, "Palabra final," *Historia de una escalera*, p. 156.

13. Buero Vallejo, *El tragaluz* (Madrid: Ediciones Alfil, 1968), p. 11.

14. Ángel Fernández-Santos, "Una entrevista con Buero Vallejo," *Primer Acto*, No. 90 (September, 1967), p. 11.

15. In "Las dificultades de mi puesta en escena de *El tragaluz*," José Osuna explains that the pitlike sensation which the text refers to insistently was heightened by constructing a platform inclining at a twenty degree angle and by situating the bar and Vicente's office on slightly higher levels. Buero Vallejo, *Teatro*, Colección el Mirlo Blanco No. 10 (Madrid: Taurus Ediciones, 1968), p. 105.

16. A. Fernández-Santos, "El enigma de *El tragaluz*," *Primer Acto*, No. 90 (September, 1967), pp. 4-5.

17. In A. Fernández-Santos, "Una entrevista con Buero Vallejo," pp. 13-14.

18. *Ibid.*, p. 12.

19. José María de Quinto, "*El tragaluz*, de Buero Vallejo," *Insula*, No. 252 (November, 1968), p. 15.

20. Ricardo Doménech, "A propósito de *El tragaluz*," from *Cuadernos para el diálogo*, No. 51 (December, 1967), reprinted in Buero Vallejo, *Teatro* (Madrid: Taurus Ediciones, 1968), p. 126.

21. José María de Quinto (see note 19) remarks, perhaps with a bit of exaggeration, that, "in a certain sense, Mario belongs to that 'underground' which Dostoevski describes as a substratum of demoniacal and uncontrollable evil. Impelled by a secret recondite rancor, he involuntarily does everything possible to precipitate his brother Vicente into the abyss."

22. There are numerous indications that the vision through the basement window corresponds to reality. Vicente, for example, sees, or imagines he sees, the figure of Beltrán, one of his victims, and overhears a refusal to recognize an illegitimate child made in exactly the same words with which he replied to Encarna.

23. See Lorenzo López Sánchez, "*El tragaluz*, de Buero Vallejo, en el teatro Bellas Artes," *ABC* (October 10, 1967), pp. 111-12, and Doménech, "A propósito de *El tragaluz*," p. 127.

24. Ricardo Doménech speculates that the father may represent God, although he does not state this definitively. He points out that when the mother and sons cannot answer the father's question "Who is that?" the latter insists that he knows the answer—an answer which, Vicente has stated, can be known from God's point of view. The father, moreover, states that he asks only in order to test his sons. In Vicente's words, "He believes he is God." Vicente, furthermore, states that he confesses before his father as if in the presence of God. Thereupon the father reacts, in Doménech's words, "like a terrible avenging god." "He is a strange, fascinating and ambiguous figure," the critic adds, "like Beckett's Godot. But with a very important difference: this Godot *has come* and he has come to punish." See Doménech, "*El tragaluz*, una tragedia de nuestro tiempo," *Cuadernos Hispanoamericanos*, No. 217 (January, 1968), pp. 132-33.

25. *Ibid.*, p. 134.

26. In A. Fernández-Santos, "Una entrevista con Buero Vallejo," p. 8.

27. *Ibid.*, p. 10.

28. Doménech, "A propósito de *El Tragaluz*," p. 127.

29. Buero, "La ceguera en mi teatro," *La Carreta*, No. 12 (September, 1963), p. 5.

(September, 1963), p. 5.

30. Diderot discusses the remarkable accomplishments of Melanie de Salignac in the "Addition" to his "Lettres sur les Aveugles." Blind almost from birth, Melanie wrote and read music by using relief notes and bars. *Oeuvres choisies de Diderot*, I, ed. François Tulou (Paris, 1893), 103-15.

31. Buero, *The Concert at Saint Ovide*, trans. Farris Anderson, in *Modern International Drama*, I, No. 1 (September, 1967), 44-45. I have used Anderson's translation, but have changed the characters' names back into the original Spanish.

32. Ricardo Doménech, "*El concierto de San Ovidio* o una defensa del hombre," *Primer Acto*, No. 38 (December, 1962), p. 17.

33. Rafael Vázquez Zamora, "En el Goya, los trágicos ciegos de Buero Vallejo," *Ínsula*, No. 193 (December, 1962), p. 16.

34. Pedro Laín Entralgo, Review of *El concierto de San Ovidio* from *La Gaceta Ilustrada* of Madrid, reprinted in *Teatro español 1962-63*, ed. Sáinz de Robles (Madrid, 1964), p. 74.

35. Ángel Fernández-Santos, "*El concierto de San Ovidio*," *Índice*, No. 168, p. 21.

36. Doménech, "*El concierto de San Ovidio* o una defensa...," p. 17.

37. F. García Pavón, "*El concierto de San Ovidio* de Buero Vallejo," *Arriba* (November 17, 1962), p. 19.

38. de Quinto, p. 15. See note 19.

39. Tomás Zamarriego, "*El tragaluz*," *Razón y Fe*, No. 840 (January-June, 1968), pp. 26-29.

40. "Cuatro autores contestan a cuatro preguntas sobre teatro social," *Arriba* (April 14, 1963), p. 12.

41. de Quinto, p. 15.

Chapter Six

1. Madrid: Ediciones Alfil, 1970, p. 55.

2. Buero, in *Manifiesto sobre arte y libertad: encuesta entre los intelectuales y artistas españoles* (New York: Las Américas, 1963), pp. 103-4.

3. Torrente Ballester, Review of *Un soñador para un pueblo*, from *Arriba*, reprinted in *Teatro español 1958-59*, ed. Sáinz de Robles (Madrid, 1964), p. 203.

4. Buero, "Buero Vallejo nos habla," *Negro Sobre Blanco*, No. 12 (Buenos Aires, April, 1960), p. 14. Buero does not deny that his Esquilache is somewhat idealized. However Esquilache, himself, suggests some of his personal failings in the play. Nor does the play fail to suggest some of the errors of the *ilustrados*. See "Tres preguntas a Buero Vallejo," *Ínsula*, No. 147 (February 15, 1959), p. 4.

In the *Ínsula* interview, Buero states that his sources for his account of the uprising of 1766 were Carlos Fernán-Núñez' *Vida de Carlos III*, Manuel Dánvila y Collado's *Reinado de Carlos III*, and Antonio Ferrer del Río's *Historia del reinado de Carlos III*, as well as works by Feijóo, Torres Villarroel, Marañón, F. Díaz-Plaja, and Sáinz de Robles.

Notes and References   161

5. Buero, *Un soñador para un pueblo* (Madrid: Ediciones Alfil, 1959), pp. 42-43.

6. Ricardo Doménech, "*Las Meninas* o la 'intelligentsia' proscrita," *Primer Acto*, No. 19 (January, 1961), p. 8.

7. Buero, "*¿Las Meninas* es una obra necesaria?" *La Carreta*, No. 12 (Barcelona, January, 1962), p. 20.

8. Buero, *Las Meninas* (Madrid: Ediciones Alfil, 1961), p. 27.

9. Torrente Ballester, Review of *Las Meninas*, *Arriba* (December 10, 1960), p. 25.

10. Doménech, "Inciso sobre teatro," *Insula*, No. 170 (January, 1961), p. 4.

11. Borel, "Buero Vallejo: Teatro y política," *Revista de Occidente*, VI (1964), 234.

12. Torrente Ballester. See note 9.

13. See, for example, Torrente, p. 25; Fernández-Santos, Review of *Las Meninas* from *Índice*, reprinted in *Teatro Español 1960-61*, pp. 75-78; and Ricardo Doménech, "Crítica de *Las Meninas*," *Cuadernos Hispanoamericanos*, No. 133, p. 123. For Buero's own defense of his Velázquez, see "Sobre la tragedia," *Entretiens sur les Lettres et les Arts*, No. 22 (1963), p. 59. He states that Velázquez' painting proclaimed his independent spirit to those able to see it, but that it is also confirmed by his delay of a year in returning from Italy despite urgent communications from the king, his decision, unique in his time, to paint a nude Venus, as well as his defiance of members of the nobility and clergy on several other occasions which Buero lists.

14. See his *Velázquez* (Madrid, 1959).

15. Doménech, "Notas sobre *El sueño de la razón*," *Primer Acto*, No. 117 (February, 1970), p. 7.

16. Buero, *El sueño de la razón* (Madrid: Ediciones Alfil, 1970), p. 25.

17. José María Claver, "No es miedo, es tristeza," *Ya*, February 8, 1970, p. 41.

18. Mariquita is María del Rosario, daughter of Leocadia. Goya is considered to have been her father, even though he was seventy at her birth in 1814.

19. Emilio Aragonés, "Goya, pintor baturro y liberal," *La Estafeta Literaria*, No. 438 (February 15, 1970), p. 36.

20. Angel Fernández-Santos, "*El sueño de la razón* de Antonio Buero Vallejo," *Insula*, No. 280 (March, 1970), p. 15.

21. See Ángel Fernández-Santos, "Sobre *El sueño de la razón*: una conversación con Antonio Buero Vallejo," *Primer Acto*, No. 117, pp. 24-26.

22. In Angel Laborda, "El estreno de hoy," *ABC*, February 6, 1970, p. 2.

23. Kronik, "Buero Vallejo y su sueño de la razón," *El Urogallo*, Nos. 5-6 (October-November-December, 1970), p. 156.

24. While many critics consider the *Black Paintings* caprices which alleviated Goya's solitude, or even products of his mental illness, Gaspar Gómez de la Serna gives them a historical and political meaning similar to Buero's in *Goya y su España* (Madrid, 1969). Buero, himself an art critic, adds to the interpretation of several paintings, especially *Asmodea*. In several cases, he uses in the play the more accurate titles found in the *Inventory* of Brugada of 1828, which differ from the Prado titles. *Asmodea* corresponds to the Prado's *El Aquelarre* (*The Witches' Sabbath*).

25. Fernández-Santos, "Sobre *El sueño de la razón*," p. 21. Goya has other works depicting winged men, and Buero believes that this indicates that the artist thought he had actually seen them. Buero points out that not even hallucinations lack all reference to that which is real, for the forms of perceiving reality are often strange and enigmatic.

26. Buero states that his historical sources include works on Goya by Sánchez Cantón and Lafuente Ferrari, among others. See Angel Laborda, the reference of note 22. The beating of Goya and the violation of Leocadia, however, are inventions of Buero, as is Goya's letter insulting the king.

27. Buero, *Aventura en lo gris* (Madrid: Ediciones Alfil, 1964), p. 44. An earlier version of the play, which differs only slightly from the later one, was published in *Teatro: Revista Internacional de la Escena*, No. 10 (January, February, March, 1954), pp. 59-76. In "Nota del autor," in the Alfil edition, Buero explains that when authorization to perform the play (written in 1949) was denied, he decided to publish it in view of the production in Madrid in 1953 of Thierry Maulnier's *La maison de la nuit*, a play with a very similar situation and plot which was written after Buero's. Permission to produce Buero's play was granted by the censors only in 1963. For a comparison of the two plays, see Guillermo de Torre's "Dos dramas fronterizos," *Índice*, No. 97 (January, 1957), pp. 21-23. Torres considers the similarities superficial.

28. Domingo Pérez Minik, *Teatro europeo contemporáneo* (Madrid: Ediciones Guadarrama, 1961), p. 387.

29. Buero, "A propósito de *Aventura en lo gris*," in *Teatro: Revista Internacional de la Escena*, No. 10, p. 39.

30. Buero, "Dos sonetos," *Cuadernos de Agora*, Nos. 57-58 (July-August, 1961), p. 7. Translation by Robert Lima.

31. Robert Sheehan comments that, despite the description of the

war as one between nations, certain episodes and comments in the play may be related to the Spanish Civil War, and terms the play an allegory. He notes that the mention of refugees fleeing over the mountains to a neutral country to escape invaders parallels the Republicans' flight into France at the end of the Civil War, Alejandro's escape to safety with a large fortune recalls charges of Republican leaders fleeing after urging their soldiers to fight on, and the mention of "concentration camps" over the border to which the humble stream, abandoned by their supposed friends, is reminiscent of those in France. At any rate, he concludes, the play shows Buero's fundamental mistrust of war. Cf. "Censorship and Buero Vallejo's Social Consciousness," *Aquila,* I (Boston, 1969), 126-29.

32. Buero, "A propósito de," p. 38.

33. Buero, "Del Quijotismo al 'mito' de los platillos volantes," *Primer Acto,* Nos. 100-101 (November-December, 1968), pp. 73-74.

34. Buero, *Mito* (Madrid: Ediciones Alfil, 1968), p. 42. In 1967, a well-known musician proposed to Buero that they compose, together, an opera on some Spanish theme of universal significance. When plans for collabration were abandoned, Buero published the text. See "Del Quijotismo al 'mito' de los platillos volantes," p. 73.

35. See note 24 to Chapter 5. In a conversation with the author, July, 1970, Buero stated that the name "Eloy" was suggested by "Elohim," the name for God used up to Moses' time in *The Elohist,* one of the historical narratives (*ca.* 750 B.C.) incorporated into the Old Testament.

36. Translation by Robert Lima.

37. Buero, "Del Quijotismo al 'mito' . . ." Cf. note 34.

38. Sergio Nerva, Review of *Las cartas boca abajo,* from *España* (Tangiers), reprinted in Sáinz de Robles (ed.), *Teatro Español 1957-58* (Madrid, 1959), pp. 3-5.

39. Pérez Minik, pp. 383-95.

40. Borel, *El teatro de lo imposible* (Madrid, 1966), p. 258.

41. Buero, "Antonio Buero Vallejo habla de Unamuno," *Primer Acto,* No. 59 (November, 1964), pp. 19-21.

42. José Monleón, "*Mito,* un libro de Buero para una ópera," *Primer Acto,* Nos. 100-101 (November-December, 1968), p. 72.

Chapter Seven

1. Madrid: Ediciones Alfil, 1951, pp. 59-60.

2. Buero, "¿*Las Meninas* es una abro necesaria?" *La Carreta,* No. 12 (January, 1962), p. 20.

3. English translation by Robert Lima.

4. Buero, "Autocrítica," *Teatro español 1950-51,* ed. Sáinz de Robles (Madrid, 1952), pp. 99-100.

164 ANTONIO BUERO VALLEJO

5. Buero, "Comentario," *En la ardiente oscuridad*, p. 83. See note 1.

6. Eduardo Haro Tecglen, Review of *En la ardiente oscuridad* from *Informaciones*, reprinted in *Teatro español 1950-51*, p. 98.

7. Pedro Laín Entralgo, Review of *El concierto de San Ovidio* from *La Gaceta Ilustrada*, reprinted in *Teatro Español 1962-63*, ed. Sáinz de Robles (Madrid, 1964), p. 73.

8. Schevill, "Introducción," *Dos dramas de Buero Vallejo* (New York, 1967), p. 7. She specifically mentions Unamuno's *Abel Sánchez* and *La venda* (*The Blindfold*).

9. Lyon, "Introduction," *Hoy es fiesta* (London, 1964), p. 20.

10. *Ibid.*

11. Buero, "Comentario," *En la ardiente oscuridad*, p. 83.

12. Lyon, p. 25.

13. Miguel de Unamuno, *Del sentimiento trágico de la vida* (*The Tragic Sense of Life*), Buenos Aires, 1947, p. 91.

14. Lyon, p. 24.

15. Buero, "Comentario." See note 5. It is interesting to observe that this play has been published in Braille. Critical reaction to the play and an interview with Buero may be found in *Sirio* (*Revista Tiflológica*), No. 2 (1962), pp. 4-19.

16. Buero, *Irene o el tesoro* (Madrid: Ediciones Alfil, 1955), p. 30.

17. Buero, "Comentario," *Irene o el tesoro*, pp. 118-23.

18. *Ibid.*, pp. 122-23.

19. José Luis Abellán, "El tema del misterio en Buero Vallejo (Un teatro de la realidad trascendente)," *Insula*, No. 174, p. 15.

20. Rosendo Roig, S. J., "Talante trágico del teatro de Buero Vallejo," *Razón y Fe*, No. 156 (1957), pp. 363-67.

21. Carlos Muñiz, S. J., "El simbolismo religioso en el teatro de Buero Vallejo," *Proyección*, No. 37 (Granada, April, 1963), pp. 92-102.

22. Buero, "Comentario," *Irene o el tesoro*, p. 123.

Chapter Eight

1. Buero, "Sobre la tragedia," *Entretiens sur les Lettres et les Arts*, No. 22 (1963), p. 57.

2. Buero, "La tragedia," *El teatro; enciclopedia del arte escénico* (Barcelona: Editorial Noguer, S.A., 1958), p. 76.

3. Buero, *Hoy es fiesta* (Madrid: Ediciones Alfil, 1957), p. 96.

Selected Bibliography

PRIMARY SOURCES

See *Notes and References* for further bibliographical orientation. For the most complete bibliography of Buero and his theater, see John Kronik, "Antonio Buero Vallejo: a Bibliography (1949-70)" in *Hispania*, LIV, No. 4 (December, 1971), 856-68.

1. Plays by Buero (in order of performance except where publication was prior or play has not been performed. The date indicated in parentheses after the title of each play is that of the initial performance. Editions are listed chronologically, each on a separate line.)

Historia de una escalera: Drama en tres actos (1949).
    (Barcelona: José Janés, 1950.)
    In Sáinz de Robles, ed. *Teatro español 1949-50* (Madrid: Aguilar, 1951).
    With *Las palabras en la arena* (Madrid: Ediciones Alfil, 1952).
    Ed. José Sánchez (New York: Scribner's, 1955).
Las palabras en la arena: Tragedia en un acto (1949).
    With *Historia de una escalera* (Madrid: Ediciones Alfil, 1952).
    In Isabel Magaña de Schevill, ed. *Dos dramas de Buero Vallejo* (New York: Appleton-Century-Crofts, 1967). The other play is *Aventura en lo gris*.
En la ardiente oscuridad: Drama en tres actos (1950).
    (Madrid: Ediciones Alfil, 1951.)
    In Sáinz de Robles, ed. *Teatro español 1950-51* (Madrid: Aguilar, 1952).
    Ed. Samuel A. Wofsy (New York: Scribner's, 1954).
La tejedora de sueños: Drama en tres actos (1952).
    (Madrid: Ediciones Alfil, 1952.)
    In Sáinz de Robles, ed. *Teatro español 1951-52* (Madrid: Aguilar, 1953).
    Translation into English by William I. Oliver, *The Dream Weaver*, in Robert W. Corrigan, ed. *Masterpieces of the Modern Spanish Theatre* (New York: Macmillan-Collier Books, 1967).

La señal que se espera: Comedia en tres actos (1952).
(Madrid: Ediciones Alfil, 1952.)
Casi un cuento de hadas: Una glosa de Perrault, en tres actos (1952).
(Madrid: Ediciones Alfil, 1953.)
Madrugada: Episodio dramático en dos actos (1953).
(Madrid: Ediciones Alfil, 1954.)
In Sáinz de Robles, ed. *Teatro español 1953-54* (Madrid: Agui-
lar, 1955).
Ed. Donald W. Bleznick and Martha T. Halsey (Waltham,
Mass.: Blaisdell, 1969).
Aventura en lo gris: Dos actos y un sueño (1963).
In *Teatro. Revista Internacional de la Escena* (Madrid), No.
10 (January-March, 1954 [original version]).
(Madrid: Ediciones Puerta del Sol, 1955 [original version].)
(Madrid: Ediciones Alfil, 1964 [revised version].)
In Isabel Magaña de Schevill, ed. *Dos dramas de Buero Vallejo*
(New York: Appleton-Century-Crofts, 1967). The other
play is *Las palabras en la arena*.
El terror inmóvil: Fragmentos de una tragedia irrepresentable.
(Not performed.) Act II only (Madrid: Ediciones Alfil, 1954).
Irene o el tesoro: Fábula en tres actos (1954).
(Madrid: Ediciones Alfil, 1955.)
In Sáinz de Robles, ed. *Teatro español 1954-55* (Madrid: Agui-
lar, 1956).
Hoy es fiesta: Tragicomedia en tres actos (1956).
(Madrid: Ediciones Alfil, 1957.)
In Sáinz de Robles, ed. *Teatro español 1956-57* (Madrid: Agui-
lar, 1958).
Ed. J. E. Lyon (London: Harrap, 1964). Reprinted by D. C.
Heath (Boston, 1966).
*Las cartas boca abajo: Tragedia española en dos partes y cuatro
cuadros* (1957).
(Madrid: Ediciones Alfil, 1968.)
In Sáinz de Robles, ed. *Teatro español 1957-58* (Madrid: Agui-
lar, 1959).
Ed. Félix G. Ilárraz (Englewood Cliffs, N. J.: Prentice Hall,
1967).
*Un soñador para un pueblo: Versión libre de un episodio histórico,
en dos partes* (1958).
(Madrid: Ediciones Alfil, 1959.)
In Sáinz de Robles, ed. *Teatro español 1958-59* (Madrid: Agui-
lar, 1960).
Ed. M. Manzanares de Cirre (New York: Norton, 1966).

Las Meninas: Fantasía velazqueña en dos partes (1960).
  In *Primer Acto,* No. 19 (Madrid, January, 1961).
  (Madrid: Ediciones Alfil, 1961.)
  In Sáinz de Robles, ed. *Teatro español 1960-61* (Madrid: Aguilar, 1962).
  Ed. Juan R. Castellano (New York: Scribner's, 1963).
El concierto de San Ovidio: Parábola en tres actos (1962).
  In *Primer Acto,* No. 38 (Madrid, December, 1962).
  (Madrid: Ediciones Alfil, 1963.)
  Ed. J.-P. Borel (Barcelona: Aymá, 1963).
  In Sáinz de Robles, ed. *Teatro español 1962-63* (Madrid: Aguilar, 1964).
  Ed. Pedro N. Trakas (New York: Scribner's, 1965).
  Translation into English by Farris Anderson, *The Concert at Saint Ovide,* in *Modern International Drama,* I (Pennsylvania State University Press, 1967). Reprinted in Marion Holt, ed. *The Modern Spanish Stage. Four Plays* (New York: Hill and Wang, 1970).
La doble historia del doctor Valmy: Relato escénico en dos partes (1968—performed in English).
  In *Artes Hispánicas,* I, No. 2 (Indiana University, 1967 [Spanish and English texts. Translation by Farris Anderson]).
  Ed. Alfonso M. Gil (Philadelphia: The Center for Curriculum Development, 1970).
El tragaluz: Experimento en dos partes (1967).
  In *Primer Acto,* No. 90 (Madrid, November, 1967).
  (Madrid: Ediciones Alfil, 1968.)
  In Sáinz de Robles, ed. *Teatro español 1967-68* (Madrid: Aguilar, 1969).
  With *El sueño de la razón* (Madrid: Espasa-Calpe, 1970. Colección Austral).
Mito: Libro para una ópera. (Not performed.)
  (Madrid: Ediciones Alfil, 1968.)
  In *Primer Acto,* No. 100-101 (Madrid, November-December, 1968).
El sueño de la razón: Fantasía en dos actos (1970).
  In *Primer Acto,* No. 117 (Madrid, February, 1970).
  (Madrid: Escelicer, 1970.)
  With *El tragaluz* (Madrid: Espasa-Calpe, 1970. Colección Austral).

2. Collections of Plays by Buero

Teatro, I: En la ardiente oscuridad. Madrugada. Hoy es fiesta. Las cartas boca abajo (Buenos Aires: Losada, 1959).

Teatro, II: Historia de una escalera. La tejedora de sueños. Irene o el tesoro. Un soñador para un pueblo (Buenos Aires: Losada, 1962).
Teatro selecto: Historia de una escalera. Las cartas boca abajo. Un soñador para un pueblo. Las Meninas. El concierto de San Ovidio. Ed. Luce Moreau-Arrabal (Madrid: Escelicer, 1966).
Teatro: Hoy es fiesta. Las Meninas. El tragaluz (Madrid: Taurus, 1968).

3. Essays by Buero

"A propósito de *Aventura en lo gris,*" *Teatro: Revista Internacional de la Escena* (Madrid), No. 9 (September-December, 1953), pp. 37-40.

"A propósito de Brecht," *Insula,* Nos. 200-201 (July-August, 1963), pp. 1-2, 14.

"Antonio Buero Vallejo Answers Seven Questions," *Theatre Annual,* 1962, pp. 1-6. The state of the theater in Spain after the Spanish Civil War and problems faced by playwrights.

"Antonio Buero Vallejo habla de Unamuno," *Primer Acto,* No. 59 (November, 1964), pp. 19-21. Unamuno, tragedy, and quixotism.

"Autocrítica" to *Story of a Stairway, In the Burning Darkness, The Dream Weaver, Dawn,* and *Irene or the Treasure* in the volumes of Sáinz de Robles, ed. *Teatro español,* in which the texts of the plays appear—as cited above.

"Buero Vallejo nos habla de *Hoy es fiesta* y *Un soñador para un pueblo,*" *Negro sobre Blanco: Boletín Literario Bibliográfico,* No. 12 (Buenos Aires: Editorial Losada S. A., April, 1960), pp. 1-2, 14.

"La ceguera en mi teatro," *La Carreta* (Barcelona), No. 12 (September, 1963), p. 5.

"Comentario" to *Almost a Fairy Tale, In the Burning Darkness, Dawn, The Dream Weaver, Irene or the Treasure, The Awaited Sign, Today's a Holiday* and *The Words in the Sand* in the Alfil edition of each play cited above.

"¿Cómo recibió su premio?" *Índice,* No. 50 (April 15, 1952), p. 6. Re *Story of a Stairway.*

"Cuatro autores contestan a cuatro preguntas sobre teatro social," *Arriba* (April 14, 1963), p. 12. Also includes statements by Alfonso Paso, Alfonso Sastre, and Lauro Olmo.

"Cuidado con la amargura," *Correo Literario* (Madrid), No. 2 (June 15, 1950), pp. 8-9. The positive nature of tragedy with specific reference to *Story of a Stairway.*

"Del Quijotismo al 'mito' de los platillos volantes," *Primer Acto,* Nos. 100-101 (November-December, 1968), pp. 73-74. Commentary to *Myth.*

"De rodillas, en pie, en el aire (Sobre el autor y sus personajes en el teatro de Valle-Inclán)," *Revista de Occidente,* Nos. 44-45 (1966), pp. 132-45. Humanizing emotion and cathartic effects in the *esperpentos* or farces of Valle-Inclán.

"Me llamo Antonio Buero Vallejo." Madrid: Discos Aguilar, 1964 (phonograph record). Basic introduction to Buero and his ideas on the theater.

"¿*Las Meninas* es una obra necesaria?" *La Carreta* (Barcelona), No. 2 (January, 1962), p. 20. Parallels between *The Ladies-in-Waiting* and Buero's other theater.

"Palabra final," *Historia de una escalera.* Ed. José Janés (Barcelona, 1950), pp. 149-57.

"Un poema y un recuerdo," *Insula,* No. 168 (November, 1960), pp. 1, 17. Reminiscences about Buero's friendship with Miguel Hernández.

"Problemas del teatro actual," *Boletín de la Sociedad General de Autores de España,* April-May-June, 1970, pp. 31-36. The theaters of participation and alienation. Physical versus psychic participation and remarks on *Hair.*

"Sobre la tragedia," *Entretiens sur les Lettres et les Arts* (Rodez, France), No. 22 (1963), pp. 52-61. Important statement of Buero's conception of tragedy. Comments on *The Ladies-in-Waiting.*

"El teatro de Buero Vallejo visto por Buero Vallejo," *Primer Acto,* No. 1 (April, 1597), pp. 4-6. Interesting comments on the relationship which Buero sees between his painting and his theater.

"La tragedia," *El teatro: enciclopedia del arte escénico.* Ed. Guillermo Díaz-Plaja (Barcelona: Editorial Noguer, 1958), pp. 63-87. Most complete statement of Buero's ideas on tragedy.

"Tres preguntas a Buero Vallejo," *Insula,* No. 147 (February 15, 1959), p. 4. Remarks about *A Dreamer for a People.*

4. Interviews with Buero

BAQUERO, ARCADIO. "Buero Vallejo, pintor," *La Estafeta Literaria,* No. 198 (August 9, 1960), pp. 14-15. Discussion of the drawings and paintings by Buero kept in his apartment study.

DULSEY, BERNARD. "Entrevista a Buero Vallejo," *The Modern Language Journal,* L, No. 3 (March, 1966), 145-56. Remarks about contemporary Spanish novelists, modern European and American playwrights, recent currents in art and music, literary and philosophical influences acknowledged by Buero, and his concept of tragedy.

FERNÁNDEZ CUENCA, CARLOS. "El autor y su obra preferida," *Correo*

Literario, No. 69 (1953), pp. 10, 12. Re the genesis of *Story of a Stairway* and *In the Burning Darkness*.

FERNÁNDEZ-SANTOS, ÁNGEL. "Una entrevista con Buera Vallejo sobre *El tragaluz*," *Primer Acto*, No. 90 (September, 1967), pp. 7-15.

——————. "Sobre *El sueño de la razón*: una conversación con Antonio Buero Vallejo," *Primer Acto*, No. 117 (February, 1970), pp. 18-27.

FRAILE, MEDARDO. "Charla con Antonio Buero Vallejo," *Cuadernos de Agora*, Nos. 79-82 (May-August, 1963), pp. 4-8. General comments on Buero's own theater, his writing habits, and his preferences among modern authors.

LABORDA, ÁNGEL. "El estreno de hoy," *ABC* (February 6, 1970), pp. 71-72. About *The Sleep of Reason*.

MARQUERÍE, ALFREDO. "Los autores ante su estreno," *La Estafeta Literaria*, No. 105 (November 23, 1957), pp. 1, 2. About *The Cards Face Down*.

MARRA-LÓPEZ, JOSÉ R. "Conversación con Antonio Buero Vallejo," *Cuadernos del Congreso por la Libertad de la Cultura* (Paris), No. 42 (May-June, 1960), pp. 55-58. Comments on the significance of tragedy, *A Dreamer for a People*, and literary influences on his theater.

MONTERO, ISAAC. "Una baraja en tres posturas," *La Estafeta Literaria*, No. 105 (November 23, 1957), pp. 8-10. About *The Cards Face Down*.

PAJÓN MECLOY, ERIQUE. "Hablando con Buero Vallejo," *Sirio* (Madrid), No. 2 (April, 1962), pp. 4-5. About *In the Burning Darkness* and the significance of blindness in Buero's theater.

PÉREZ DE OLAGUER, GONZALO. "Antonio Buero Vallejo, nuevo académico de la lengua," *Yorick* (Barcelona), No. 46 (March, 1971), pp. 5-10. Buero's reaction to his election to the Royal Academy and comments upon the evolution of his theater.

RODRÍGUEZ, MIGUEL LUIS. "Diálogo con Antonio Buero Vallejo," *Índice*, Nos. 116-17 (September-October, 1958), pp. 21-22; No. 118 (October, 1958), pp. 22-23; No. 119 (December, 1958), pp. 19-20. Buero's concept of "symbolic realism" with special reference to *The Cards Face Down*. The social role of his theater.

SARTO, JUAN DEL. "Pasado, presente y porvenir del escritor en España," *Correo Literario*, No. 52 (July 15, 1952), p. 3. Buero's theatrical experimentation as a young child.

TRENAS, JULIO. "Buero Vallejo, en y ante el teatro moderno," *ABC* (June 4, 1969), pp. 124-25, 129. Formal problems in the theater, including participation and distancing.

SECONDARY SOURCES

ABELLÁN, JOSÉ LUIS. "El tema del misterio en Buero Vallejo," *Ínsula*, No. 174 (May, 1961), p. 15. The search for a transcendent reality.

ARAGONÉS, JUAN EMILIO. "Antonio Buero Vallejo," *La Estafeta Literaria*, No. 462 (February 15, 1971), pp. 4-11. Includes bibliography of translations of Buero's plays into other languages, Buero's essays, and critical studies of his theater published outside of Spain. Photographs of Buero and his family.

ATLEE, ALFRED FRANCIS. "*Las cartas boca abajo*: clave del teatro de Buero," *Papeles de Son Armadans*, No. 175 (October, 1970), pp. 91-112. Ethical implications of *The Cards Face Down*.

————. "The Social-Political Ethic in the plays of Antonio Buero Vallejo produced and published from October 1949 to October 1963." Doctoral dissertation, Arizona, 1967. *DA*, XXVIII (1967): 2236A. The need for abnegation and generosity.

BLEZNICK, DONALD W. and HALSEY, MARTHA T. "Introduction." In *Madrugada* (Waltham, Mass.: Blaisdell Publ. Co., 1969), pp. ix-xxiv. Analysis of Buero's concept of tragedy and of *Dawn*.

BOREL, JEAN-PAUL. "Buero Vallejo." In *Quelques aspects du songe dans la littérature espagnole* (Neuchâtel, Suisse: Editions de la Baconnière, 1965), pp. 51-64. The "political dream" in *In the Burning Darkness*, *A Dreamer for a People*, and *Adventure in Gray*.

————. "Buero Vallejo o lo imposible concreto e histórico." In *El teatro de lo imposible: Ensayo sobre una de las dimensiones fundamentales del teatro español contemporáneo*. Trans. Torrente Ballester (Madrid: Ediciones Guadarrama, 1966), pp. 225-80. Penetrating analysis of Buero's plays from an existentialist viewpoint.

————. "Buero Vallejo: Teatro y Política," *Revista de Occidente*, VI, No. 17 (1964), 226-34. Political implications of *In the Burning Darkness* and *Concert at Saint Ovide*.

CERUTTI, LUCIA M. "Interpretazione del teatro di Antonio Buero Vallejo," *Aevum* (Milan, May-August, 1966), pp. 315-64. The evolution of dreams in Buero's theater. Extensive bibliography.

CORTINA, JOSÉ R. *El arte dramático de Antonio Buero Vallejo* (Madrid: Editoral Gredos, 1969). Basic introduction to Buero's theater through 1964. Doctoral dissertation. Illinois, 1967. See *DA*, XXVIII (1968), 3174A-75A.

DONAHUE, FRANCIS. "Spain's Theater of Commitment," *Books Abroad*, Summer, 1969, pp. 354-58. Social commitment in *Story of a Stairway*, *Today's a Holiday*, and *The Basement Window*.

FERNÁNDEZ-TORRIENTE, GASTÓN. "España en el teatro social de Antonio Buero Vallejo." Doctoral dissertation, U. of Miami, 1968. *DA,* XXIX (1968), 1893A. Spain in Buero's (1) "neorealistic" theater which portrays Spanish society today directly and (2) more dialectical "historical-social" theater.

GARCÍA PAVÓN, F. "Antonio Buero Vallejo: sus trabajos y sus días," *Destino,* No. 1742 (February 20, 1971), pp. 22-23. Interesting character sketch of Buero by critic who knows him well.

GIULIANO, WILLIAM. "The Role of Man and Woman in Buero Vallejo's Plays," *Hispanófila,* No. 39 (May, 1970), pp. 21-28. The success or failure of Buero's men and women characters to realize their human potential.

HALSEY, MARTHA T. "The Dreamer in the Tragic Theater of Antonio Buero Vallejo," *Revista de Estudios Hispánicos,* II, No. 2 (November, 1968), 265-85.

————. "Goya in the Theater: Buero's *El sueño de la razón,*" *Kentucky Romance Quarterly,* XVIII, No. 2 (1971), 207-21.

————. "'Light' and 'Darkness' as Dramatic Symbols in Two Tragedies of Buero Vallejo," *Hispania,* L, No. 1 (March, 1967), 63-68. About *In the Burning Darkness* and *Concert at Saint Ovide.*

————. "The Tragedies of Antonio Buero Vallejo." Doctoral dissertation, Ohio State, 1964. *DA,* XXV (1965), 5278-79. Buero's theater as a search for truth. Tragedy, the symbolism of light and darkness, the dreamer-protagonist, and hope.

ILARRAZ, FÉLIX. "Antonio Buero Vallejo: ¿Pesimismo o esperanza?" *Revista de Estudios Hispánicos,* I, No. 1 (1967), 5-16. Positive nature of Buero's tragedies.

KRONIK, JOHN W. "Cela, Buero y la generación de 1936: raigambre de una visión histórica," *Symposium,* XXII, No. 2 (Summer, 1968), 164-71. Important assessment of Buero's place in contemporary Spanish literature.

LOTT, ROBERT E. "Functional Flexibility and Ambiguity in Buero Vallejo's Plays," *Symposium,* XX, No. 2 (Summer, 1966), 150-62. Perspectivism and relativism, the ambiguities of victory and defeat, and other complexities of Buero's theater.

————. "Scandinavian Reminiscences in Antonio Buero Vallejo," *Romance Notes,* VII, No. 2 (1966), 113-16. Affinities of Buero with Strindberg and Ibsen.

LYON, J. E. "Introduction." In *Hoy es fiesta* (London: George G. Harrap & Co. Ltd., 1964); also (Boston: D. C. Heath, 1966), pp. 7-39. Concise and penetrating analysis of the general characteristics of Buero's theater and of *Today's a Holiday.*

MANZANARES, DE CIRRE. "El realismo social de Buero Vallejo," *Revista Hispánica Moderna,* XXVII (1961), 320-24. Buero's visionary tragedy, such as *A Dreamer for a People* contrasted with his socially oriented tragedies of "testimony."

MUÑIZ, CARLOS. "Antonio Buero Vallejo: Ese hombre comprometido," *Primer Acto,* No. 38 (December, 1962), pp. 8-10. The relationship between Buero, the man, and his works as seen by a fellow playwright.

MUÑIZ ROMERO, S.J., CARLOS. "El simbolismo religioso en el teatro de Buero Vallejo," *Proyección* (Granada), No. 37 (April, 1963), pp. 92-102. Buero's theater seen from a Christian existentialistic perspective.

NICHOLAS, ROBERT L. "The Evolution of Technique in the Theater of Antonio Buero Vallejo." Doctoral dissertation, Oregon, 1967. *DA,* XXIX (1968), 269A-270A. The two-phase chronological evolution of technique in Buero's plays: the early family tragedies patterned after Ibsen, and the later historical plays modeled after Brecht.

————. "The History Plays: Buero Vallejo's Experiment in Dramatic Expression," *Revista de Estudios Hispánicos,* III, No. 2 (November, 1969), 281-93. Structural development and fusion of art forms in *A Dream for a People* and *The Ladies-in-Waiting.*

O'CONNOR, PATRICIA W. "Censorship in the Contemporary Spanish Theater and Antonio Buero Vallejo," *Hispania,* LII, No. 2 (May, 1969), 282-88.

PASTOR PETIT, D. "Afinidades y antagonismos: Buero Vallejo-Dostoyewski," *La Vanguardia Española,* July 9, 1971. Parallels between characters in selected works of the two authors.

PÉREZ MINIK, DOMINGO. "Buero Vallejo o la restauración de la máscara." In *Teatro europeo contemporáneo: su libertad y compromisos* (Madrid: Ediciones Guadarrama, 1961), pp. 381-95. Buero's plays as a judgment on modern Spanish society, of which the family, with its constant discord, is a microcosm.

SCHEVILL, ISABEL MAGAÑA DE. "Introducción." In *Dos dramas de Buero Vallejo* (New York: Appleton-Century-Crofts, 1967), pp. 1-15. Buero's ethics and aesthetics. Interesting parallels between Buero and Unamuno.

————. "Lo trágico en el teatro de Buero Vallejo," *Hispanófila,* No. 7 (September, 1959), pp. 51-58. The fusion of literal and symbolic reality in *In the Burning Darkness, Today's a Holiday,* and *The Cards Face Down.*

SCHWARTZ, KESSEL. "Buero Vallejo and the Concept of Tragedy," *Hispania,* LI, No. 4 (December, 1968), 817-24. Buero's ideas on tragedy and their application to his own works.

————. "Posibilismo and Imposibilismo: The Buero Vallejo-Sastre Polemic," *Revista Hispánica Moderna*, XXXIV, No. 1-2 (January-April, 1968), 436-45. Buero's concept of an "open" tragedy of hope versus Sastre's idea of a "closed" tragedy of anguish. The problem of writing plays whose staging is possible despite censorship and commercialism.

SHEEHAN, ROBERT L. "Censorship and Buero Vallejo's Social Consciousness,' *Aquila: Chestnut Hill Studies in Modern Languages and Literatures*, I (1969), 121-37. The use of allegory, fantasy, and history in Buero's treatment of social themes.

ADDENDUM

BUERO VALLEJO, ANTONIO. *García Lorca ante el esperpento* (Madrid: Real Academia Española, 1972). Buero's speech before the Spanish Royal Academy upon being received as a member and the response by Pedro Laín Entralgo.

————. *Llegada de los dioses* (*Arrival of the Gods*). In *Primer Acto*, No. 138 (Madrid, November, 1971). Buero's most recent play premièred September 17, 1971 at the Lara Theater of Madrid.

CASA, FRANK P. "The Problem of National Reconciliation in Buero Vallejo's *El tragaluz*," *Revista Hispánica Moderna*, XXXV, No. 3 (January-April, 1969), 185-94.

FRANCOLI, EDUARDO. "La forma dramática de Bertolt Brecht y Buero Vallejo," *Reflexion 2*, I, No. 1 (Ottawa, July, 1972), 81-91.

GIULIANO, WILLIAM. *Buero Vallejo, Sastre y el teatro de su tiempo* (New York: Las Americas, 1971).

NICHOLAS, ROBERT. *The Tragic Stages of Antonio Buero Vallejo* (Chapel Hill: University of North Carolina Press, 1972). Estudios de Hispanófila, 23.

ROEPLE, JOELYN. *Antonio Buero Vallejo: The First Fifteen Years* (New York: Eliseo Torres, 1972).

Index

175